Blind No More

Mercer University Lamar Lectures No. 57

BLIND NO MORE
African American Resistance, Free-Soil Politics, and the Coming of the Civil War

JONATHAN DANIEL WELLS

THE UNIVERSITY OF GEORGIA PRESS   Athens

Paperback edition, 2021
© 2019 by the University of Georgia Press
Athens, Georgia 30602
www.ugapress.org
All rights reserved
Set in 10.3/15 Sabon and ITC Century by Rebecca A. Norton

Most University of Georgia Press titles are
available from popular e-book vendors.

Printed digitally

The Library of Congress has cataloged the
hardcover edition of this book as follows:
Names: Wells, Jonathan Daniel, 1969– author.
Title: Blind no more : African American resistance, free-soil politics, and the coming of the Civil War / Jonathan Daniel Wells.
Description: Athens, Georgia : The University of Georgia Press, [2019] | Includes bibliographical references and index.
Identifiers: LCCN 2018036509 | ISBN 9780820354859 (hardcover : alk. paper) Subjects: LCSH: United States. Fugitive slave law (1850) | Fugitive slaves—Legal status, laws, etc.—United States. | Slavery—Political aspects—United States—History—19th century.
Classification: LCC E450 .W46 2019 | DDC 342.7308/7—dc23
LC record available at https://lccn.loc.gov/2018036509

Paperback ISBN 978-0-8203-6036-2

For David R. Colburn
mentor and friend

From the day you disappear I dream and plot. To learn where you are and how to be there. I want to run across the trail through the beech and white pine but I am asking myself which way? Who will tell me? Who lives in the wilderness between this farm and you and will they help me or harm me?

—TONI MORRISON, *A Mercy*

Contents

Foreword, by Douglas E. Thompson xi
Acknowledgments xv

INTRODUCTION
1

CHAPTER 1
The Long Civil War: Kidnapping and Black Activists in the Early Republic
14

CHAPTER 2
The Making of the Fugitive Slave Law and the Sectional Crisis
43

CHAPTER 3
Civil Conflict in the North: Reactions to the Fugitive Slave Law in the Fall of 1850
71

CHAPTER 4
Trying to Save the Union: Battles over the Fugitive Slave Law in the 1850s
90

CHAPTER 5
An End to Compromise
115

Notes 135
Index 163

Foreword

In late October 2017, Jonathan D. Wells gave the Eugenia Dorothy Blount Lamar Lectures at Mercer University. For the first time in the series' sixty-year history, a lecturer turned the gaze away from the American South to examine how the regional divide leading to the American Civil War occurred because of the radicalizing political influence of African Americans—those who escaped to free soil and those born on free soil—on the abolitionist movement. Wells places African Americans at the center of the regional crisis rather than branding them as passive subjects of southern politicians and white northern abolitionists in the slide toward civil war. The Lamar committee is grateful to Wells for redirecting southern studies' attention in this way.

In the mid-1950s, Eugenia Dorothy Blount Lamar made a bequest to Mercer University, located in her hometown of Macon, Georgia, "to provide lectures of the very highest scholarship which will aid in the permanent preservation of the values of Southern culture, history, and literature." For sixty years, the Lamar Memorial Lectures committee has brought to Mercer the best minds to examine and explain the peculiar politics, social customs, religious piety, and racial dynamics of the American South. In that sixty-year history, scholars of history and literature have revealed the complexity of the region, perhaps sometimes even in contrast to Lamar's own understanding of the "permanent preservation of the values of Southern culture." In the case of Well's lectures, he treated the committee, Mercer's undergraduates, and the wider Macon community to a series of lectures that allowed enslaved people and former enslaved people to tell the story of their role in the coming Civil War.

Since the last publication of the Lamar Memorial Lecture Series, Mercer University earned a National Endowment of the Humanities (NEH) Challenge Grant, which will over the course of five years establish a $2 million endowment to underwrite the extensive programming around southern studies at the university, including the Lamar Memorial Lecture Series. In 2017, Mercer established the Spencer B. King, Jr. Center for Southern Studies to house both the endowment and southern studies programs. Named after a longtime history department faculty member, the King Center for Southern Studies fosters critical discussions about the many meanings of the South. As the only center for southern studies in the United States dedicated to the education and enrichment solely of undergraduate students, the center's primary purpose is to examine the region's complex history and culture through courses, conversations, and events that are open, honest, and accessible.

The committee would like to thank three people in particular who helped pull off both the lectures and the manuscript publication. Longtime program assistant Bobbie Shipley coordinated all of our efforts to bring this lecture series to Macon, as she has for several decades. Mick Gusinde-Duffy and Beth Snead have been wonderful guides as the three lectures turned into an introduction and five-chapter publication. I am particularly grateful to Beth for her patience and keen sense of how these published lectures will help reorient the way we think and write about the American South moving forward.

With this publication, the Lamar Memorial Lectures committee would like to acknowledge six decades of work by dedicated faculty and administrators at Mercer University to sustain this valuable series to the field of southern studies. Their constant attention to bring "the very highest scholarship" to publication is a testament to the importance of critical analysis of the region and the role it plays in the nation. Wells's lectures extended that conversation as we head toward the next sixty years.

Douglas E. Thompson, Chairman
Lamar Memorial Lecture Committee
Director, Spencer B. King, Jr. Center for Southern Studies
Macon, Georgia

Acknowledgments

I was honored to deliver the 2017 Lamar Lectures at Mercer University, and I would like to thank especially Professors Sarah E. Gardner and Doug Thompson as well as the staff of the Spencer B. King Jr. Center for Southern Studies for their warm hospitality. Many thanks as well to the University of Georgia Press and its editors and staff, including Jon Davies and Joseph Muller, for helping to improve the manuscript.

Blind No More

Introduction

Standing in the middle of Philadelphia's paean to American independence, one can easily become enthralled by the boldness and bravery of the nation's founding fathers. At Independence Mall, visitors by the hundreds of thousands endure the hot and humid summer of the Delaware Valley to learn about Benjamin Franklin, the signing of the Declaration of Independence, and the revered delegates who drafted the Constitution. Expansive and expensive modern glass-and-steel buildings sit uneasily among eighteenth-century brick colonial facades that harbor the stories of the nation's founding, as told by dedicated and knowledgeable National Park Service guides.

Just blocks away from Independence Hall and the mall stands a small plaque that tells a different, almost unknown, story of American freedom. Located along the Delaware River, the plaque recalls a vitally important tale in the nation's history. As the marker states plainly, affording its subject just a handful of lines, in 1855 Jane Johnson and two of her sons escaped a life of bondage. Brought to Philadelphia by her North Carolina master, a prominent Democratic pol who was en route to a diplomatic post in Central America, Johnson was under strict orders not to speak to anyone. Yet when her master briefly left the enslaved family locked in a hotel room, Johnson managed to slip a note to a black bellhop revealing her deep desire to escape. Soon Philadelphia's active network of black and white abolitionists, including William Still and Passmore Williamson, sprang into action, rescuing Johnson just as she and her sons were boarding a ship to New York. Johnson bravely risked her life and the lives of her children and in defiance of the Constitution's Fugitive Slave Clause fled to freedom. Yet Johnson's rich tale is largely unknown except by a few specialized scholars. The stark difference between the historical marker placed on Philadelphia's crowded waterfront and the acres of land made into a national park devoted to the founding fathers just a few blocks away shows that even after several decades of recovering African American history, the nation still struggles to appreciate the real and symbolic power of the African American experience and the place of that experience in the nation's sectional conflict.

Understanding the importance of black activism in intensifying sectional division requires placing African Americans at the center of Civil War causation. Thanks to valuable research by Steven Kantrowitz, Thavolia Glymph, Jim Downs, and others, we have a much more nuanced appreciation of the black Civil War experience on the battlefront and the home front.[1] At the same time, scholarship building on the valuable work of earlier generations of African American scholars like Benjamin Quarles and John Hope Franklin, particularly the recent work of historians such as Manisha Sinha, Erica Armstrong Dunbar, Patrick Rael, and many others, has shed light on the black experience before the war.[2]

However, scholars have been less inclined to link the black experience directly to causation, choosing to emphasize African American activism within the context of abolitionism. In examining the ubiquity of kidnapping and its legal counterpart in recovering fugitive slaves, we bring together two historiographies that rarely speak to one another: the coming of the war and the history of African American political activism. By pressing the political and legal system to protect their civil liberties, by keeping the issue of kidnapping at the forefront of white and black abolitionism, and by appealing to the sympathies of the white press in the free states, African Americans forced white Americans to determine what "free soil" really meant and helped bring the national crisis over slavery to civil war.

Even before 1865 witnessed both the end of the Civil War and the demise of slavery, Americans began struggling to comprehend the war's causes. All knew, as Lincoln remarked in his Second Inaugural Address, that slavery was "somehow the cause of the war," but what role precisely slavery played in sparking the conflict has been the subject of impassioned debate ever since the firing of shots at Fort Sumter began the war in April 1861. School children and scholars alike have sought to answer the same basic questions: How could Americans have come to believe that civil war was the only option left before them? How important was slavery in causing the war? Why did the conflict break out in 1861 rather than earlier or later? Was the war inevitable, or was deadly combat the result of blundering by a generation of inept and uncompromising political leaders?[3]

Generations of Americans have learned that the Compromise of 1850 narrowly averted a national political crisis when the great statesman Henry Clay stewarded the laws through Congress. Only the deft political maneuvering of the "Great Compromiser," as Clay was known for having crafted similar settlements between the North and South in 1820 and 1833, saved the Union from plunging into the abyss of civil war in 1850. The precarious but potent Compromise of 1850, historians have told us, salved the sectional wounds inflicted by decades of hostile debates over slavery. As a result of the compromise's soothing effect, northern and southern extremists retreated and relative sectional peace reigned until the fight over slavery in Kansas and Nebraska erupted in the middle of the 1850s, followed by further death blows to the Union like the *Dred Scott* Supreme Court case in 1857 and John Brown's 1859 raid on Harpers Ferry.

This story, however, is at best only partially correct. Rather than pacify the North and South, or force powerful antislavery and proslavery forces into retreat, the Compromise of 1850 brought those activists to the forefront as never before, especially in the North. As R. J. M. Blackett, Susan-Mary Grant, Michael Landis, and Leonard Richards have argued, the Fugitive Slave Act of 1850 seemed to make northern citizens complicit in the return of suspected runaway slaves, lending greater credence among ordinary northerners to abolitionist cries that a "slaveholder conspiracy" had taken hold in the federal government.[4] In his important new study, Blackett in particular argues that the Fugitive Slave Law dramatically worsened sectional relations as soon as it became public in the fall of 1850. Northern citizens, particularly adherents to the Whig and Republican Parties, were coming to believe that the phrase "slave power" was more than just a radical abolitionist slogan; it was an increasingly credible description of a political and legal system intended to employ the powers of the federal government to protect slavery and violate the rights of free states to keep bondage out of their borders.

Rather than alleviate sectional tensions, the Compromise of 1850 and especially the Fugitive Slave Law laid bare the very real divisions between North and South in new and potent ways. The law radicalized northerners, many of whom realized for the first time that no legitimate compromise with slaveholders was possible. Picking up their morning newspapers and reading about northerners rescuing and hiding runaway slaves, white southerners concluded with equal conviction that the Yankees were determined to circumvent the Constitution as well as laws passed by the federal government. Reaction to the law, which continued to ignite controversy throughout the 1850s, rendered civil war much more likely.

When explaining the sectional crisis or the coming of the Civil War, historians often emphasize the evolution of southern ideology over the early decades of the nineteenth century, especially the hardening of proslavery ideology after Nat Turner's Revolt in Virginia in 1831. Scholars trace the shift in southern political thought toward a much more intolerant and intransigent view that slavery was not just a burden placed on nineteenth-century Americans by the colonial legacy of bondage, not just a relic from a previous era, but a positive good to society. The hardening of this southern position, historians maintain, worsened the sectional crisis and moved the region toward a clash with the free labor North and Midwest.

There is no doubt that white southerners, particularly political and legal leaders, became more steadfast in their defense of slavery by the 1850s. Until the later antebellum period, it had been possible to declare slavery a detriment to the region's economy, and in the immediate aftermath of Nat Turner's Rebellion, Virginia state legislators spent weeks debating the merits and problems of southern slavery, but those debates would be the last substantial questioning of the future of bondage in the American South; in the last three antebellum decades white southerners became violently intolerant of anyone who dared to undermine the moral or legal legitimacy of slavery.

Less often studied by scholars of nineteenth-century America is the fact that antebellum northerners and midwesterners also experienced a dramatic shift in opinion, seen not just in the growth of the antislavery movement and the emergence of free labor ideology but through a fundamental change in their willingness to adhere to the constitutional compromise on which the Union had been erected. As historian Michael Woods has recently noted, central to this change in northern public opinion was the embrace of a northern version of the states' rights ideology that often is solely applied to the South.[5] Antebellum northerners had to decide: Was slavery a national obligation, as the Constitution clearly stated in its requirement that runaways be returned, or did northern communities have the right to set their own local and state laws prohibiting slavery and the return of fugitives?

Such a debate turns the traditional view of federal and states' rights on its head: northern Democrats, abandoning their foundational notion, inherited from the age of Jefferson and continued by the followers of Andrew Jackson, favored limited government. They called for an active and powerful federal apparatus to ensure the return of the self-emancipated, regardless of state or local laws outlawing bondage, a call that became the Fugitive Slave Law of 1850. On the other hand, northern Whigs and then Republicans not only advocated the preeminence of local laws that prohibited the existence of slavery, which every northern and midwestern state had stipulated by 1830, but also used a series of state "liberty laws" to render the return of runaways illegal.

Demonstrating that the powerful hand of the plantation South reached into the North does not obscure the important work of black and white abolitionists who staked their very lives on the defeat of bondage. Scholars have shown clearly how the remarkable bravery on the part of courageous abolitionists contributed mightily to the end of slavery in 1865.[6] From the perspective of African Americans, though, as appreciative as they could be of abolitionist exertions on their behalf, the Unionist hegemony that sought to preserve the constitutional compact at the expense of black civil rights blurred the line between free and slave states, erasing the fragile boundaries between "societies with slaves" and "slave societies" that white political leaders struggled to maintain.[7]

There are many valuable historical examinations of the war's origins, and virtually all point to slavery as the central cause of the conflict. Yet, as Chandra Manning has argued in *What This Cruel War Was Over*, to highlight the importance of bondage is "to open rather than solve a mystery."[8] Indeed, scholars have increasingly sought to understand the evolution of ideology in the antebellum free states, when Americans living on free soil engaged in internal political battles over the importance of protecting the rights of slaveholders as the price of maintaining the Union. As historian Adam I. P. Smith has recently argued in *The Stormy Present*, the conflicts free-state citizens had to confront in the early nineteenth century were "issues that most would rather not have had to deal with." The conservative majority living in the free states, though, had no choice but to face the key conflict handed down by the founders: how to deal with the Constitution's various compromises over slavery.[9]

We often revere in American "civil religion" the prescient genius of the so-called founding generation. Out of the Constitutional Convention held in the sweltering summer of 1787 came a remarkable document, remarkable as much for what it failed to do as what it managed to accomplish in setting up a democratic republic with coequal branches of government and a system of checks and balances designed to promote stability. In fact, the document that emerged from the deliberations in Philadelphia was a deeply flawed compromise that created structural weaknesses and delayed major controversies for future generations to confront. It is true that founders like James Madison developed new ways to think about how democracies might function in a nation as geographically large as the young United States, a case he made eloquently in *The Federalist Papers*. But Madison and the other founders were men, and not gods, whatever our civil religion might tell us. In many ways, as we will see, the flaws inherent in the Constitution doomed the young republic to failure.

Of course, the founding fathers did not consciously establish a Union that they knew was doomed to collapse, but one might well argue that the American Civil War was a foreseeable conflict given the decisions made in the Philadelphia convention. This is not to say that one could have predicted the timing and precise circumstance of that great conflict; chance, political decisions large and small, and the accumulated actions of tens of thousands of enslaved people who risked all to emancipate themselves by running toward freedom—all of these and other matters would determine the outbreak of war in April 1861. But our modern reluctance to admit that the war was inevitable has led us too often to rely on happenstance in explaining the coming of the war. I will aim to help remedy that reluctance in the pages that follow.

That the Constitution protected and defended slavery, placing on the shoulders of future generations the impossible task of maintaining a house divided between bondage and freedom, was the consequence of compromise between northern and southern interests. The document itself, as historians often point out, does not contain the words "slave" or "slavery"; the authors chose instead to employ euphemisms like "those bound to service." Perhaps this obfuscation reflected an acknowledgment of the contradictions in establishing a democratic government that relied so heavily on the continuance of slavery. If so, the pangs of conscience were not so powerful as to prevent the document from embracing a deeply flawed and ultimately ill-fated compromise between slavery and freedom. As African American activist H. Ford Douglas of Cleveland declared, "I hold, sir, that the Constitution of the United States is pro-slavery, considered so by those who framed it, and construed to that end ever since its adoption."[10] The pages that follow take Douglas's claim as a truism that doomed the Union to failure.

The Constitution, and indeed our entire political processes from the president down to the neighborhood watch, is based on compromise. In our day of political rhetoric and partisanship, "compromise" tends to be a dirty word, much as it was on the eve of the Civil War. That need for political compromise emanates from the Constitutional Convention itself. As scholars have argued, the Constitution granted a number of concessions to southern slaveholders, including the three-fifths clause and the guaranteed continuance of the international slave trade for the following two decades.[11] But for our purposes the Fugitive Slave Clause will hold particular importance, and the chapters that follow will point to the crisis over fugitive slaves as fundamental to the causes of the Civil War. As northern states and northwestern territories were already beginning to jettison their colonial slave legacies, creating a powerful lure for the enslaved who yearned for freedom, the risk of enslaved peoples running away from bondage was of great concern to the founding fathers. Though by definition exact numbers in the colonial era are difficult to conjure, nonetheless it is clear that enough enslaved people emancipated themselves to render the return of runaways a requisite feature of the constitutional compromise.

Enslaved people, as we will see, were undeterred by the Constitution's Fugitive Slave Clause, and their hunger for liberty would shape the course of the nation's politics from 1787 to 1861. In fact, as historian John Ashworth has argued, by refusing to accept their lot as slaves, and by seeking every opportunity to abscond, African Americans repeatedly made a mockery of the nation's attempts to keep a divided house under one very leaky and shaky roof.[12] Generations of white political leaders from Washington to Lincoln would do their best to maintain the walls of that house—the border between slavery and freedom, between North and South—from caving in on itself. It was an impossible task.

Three factors established at the founding rendered the Union and its divided house fatally flawed. The proslavery nature of the federal Constitution represented the shaky foundation upon which the structure was erected. The Constitution was simultaneously a blueprint for an ambitious democratic government and an agreement that, in David Waldstreicher's words, "evades, legalizes, and calibrates slavery."[13] Perhaps there was no other way—perhaps there would have been no Constitution, no American Union, without the concessions to slavery. Regardless, the Union was likely imperiled from its very inception.

Two other factors endangered the Union and its future. As chapter 2 seeks to demonstrate, enslaved peoples persisted in running away, breaching that divide between slavery and freedom by the thousands and perhaps tens of thousands, and creating a cycle of action and reaction that plagued any attempts to maintain a house divided. Political leaders at the local and national level were unable to solve the massive problem of African Americans who ran away from slavery. It was a problem that vexed politicians and tore the nation apart.

The Constitution's Fugitive Slave Clause was so ineffective that every generation of political leaders before the Civil War had to contend with the problem of runaways, efforts that culminated in the notorious Fugitive Slave Law of 1850, part of a series of measures known collectively as the Compromise of 1850, a desperate and ill-conceived set of laws that tried to solve the sectional crisis over slavery in one fell swoop and included one of the worst laws ever passed by Congress. But we should give credit where it is due: all of the fugitive slave measures from the constitutional clause to the 1850 law failed because people of color rendered them impossible to maintain. The laws failed because enslaved people refused to abide by them and ran away by any and all means they could muster: jumping on railroads, bribing steamboat captains to let them ride aboard, stowing away on ships, walking hundreds of miles, even mailing themselves, as Henry "Box" Brown did when he packed himself in a crate with some water and tremendous fearlessness. Self-emancipation was a constant earthquake that shook the foundations of the Union's hastily constructed house, and it was only a matter of time before the aftershocks wrecked it all.

A third, equally powerful problem, plagued the Union almost from its origin. Beginning with the Louisiana Purchase in 1803, the border separating freedom and slavery stretched a thousand of miles from the Atlantic shores to far beyond the Mississippi River. The gaping holes in the border allowed people of color to escape bondage, but they also permitted slaveholders and their slave-hunting agents to track down runaways. Indeed, as Matthew Salafia has argued, in the western lands along the Ohio River, whites on both sides benefited from the fact that the border was fluid, porous, and difficult to police.[14] That physical ambiguity allowed whites to hire cheap black and white labor, creating a cross-border economy that really had little interest in any kind of hard and fast wall between slavery and free soil. And while the legal trade could prosper under such ambiguity, the constant back-and-forth across the Ohio River made a mockery of the constitutional barrier that was supposed to keep slavery and free soil distinct, a liminal space that allowed an illegal economy to flourish as well. As we will see, kidnappers crossed into free territory with almost no fear of reprisal, whisking away black people and selling them as slaves. The magnitude of the problem of kidnapping has too long been obscured, despite the popularity of Solomon Northup's story *Twelve Years a Slave*.

The border between slavery and freedom was simply too long, too complex, and too varied to be policed. The constant travel across the divide, rendered all the easier by the building of every new canal, road, and railroad, meant that even as the nation matured, it was undermining its ability to sustain itself. Many scholars, from Scott Hancock to Stanley Harrold and most recently Christopher Phillips, have studied the tremendous conflicts along the extensive boundary between slave and free soil, conflicts that rise (in Harrold's words) to the level of an enduring simmering "border war." And "war" is not too strong a word. No, we did not yet have hundred-thousand-strong armies on immense battlefields; those conflicts would not come until 1861. But the hundreds of small conflicts, complete with armed conflict and killing, spies and traitors, heroic deeds and acts of cowardice, meant that long before 1861, American communities—especially those along the precarious boundary between slavery and freedom—were being ripped apart by the turmoil caused by runaways.[15]

At the center of this story are enslaved people themselves, who, in refusing to accept bondage, crossed the borders set up by political and legal authorities to keep the Union together. Following closely on their heels were slave hunters who earned rewards for recapturing the self-emancipated and kidnappers who cared little whether or not a black person was born free or slave. By seizing people of color from free soil and selling them into slavery, kidnappers made themselves wealthy even as they reminded judges and politicians that the border was impossible to secure. States took each other to court over runaways, and the federal government ultimately proved inadequate to the task of keeping order, since with each passing day, runaways, kidnappers, and slave catchers across the hundreds of miles of borders with ease.

As the fight over the Fugitive Slave Act shows, African Americans struggled mightily and persistently, often using armed resistance, to thwart the recapture of runaways. They openly and defiantly questioned the nation's commitment to basic principles of fairness and humanity, and they chastised white Americans for failing to live up to the professions of equality in the Declaration of Independence. Especially troubling for African Americans was the abrogation of fundamental rights to a trial by jury and habeas corpus, often the only two rights they could count on in a system heavily stacked against them. To an extent still unappreciated by modern readers, black northerners and southerners articulated a rights-based attack on the Fugitive Slave Law.

While African Americans defied politicians' calls for cooperation, the Fugitive Slave Act also sparked a profound and wide-ranging debate among northern whites who shunned abolition but angrily resented the law. Since the law placed the burden of returning fugitives on free states, it sparked a fundamental debate within northern communities over the duties of the individual to obey unjust laws. Spurred by the controversy over the Fugitive Slave Law, Americans engaged in a wide-ranging debate over the meaning of "rights," "liberties," and "conscience" not seen since the debates over the Constitution. Supporters and detractors of the law debated the definition of treason as well as the meaning of civil disobedience. No understanding of the causes of the Civil War or of the evolution of American freedom can be complete without an appreciation of the sermons that rang out from northern pulpits or the speeches ordinary blacks and whites delivered against the law. Far from relaxing sectional tensions as Clay and others had hoped, the law caused Americans to rethink fundamental questions. The answers Americans found did not draw the North and South together. Instead the answers drove the nation farther apart and helped convince leaders in both sections that civil war was the only remaining option.

Introduction 13

CHAPTER ONE

The Long Civil War

Kidnapping and Black Activists in the Early Republic

One day in 1827, a racially mixed crowd gathered around Seymour Cunningham on a Boston street. Cunningham had been enslaved in Alexandria, Virginia, but like thousands of others he risked his life to run away, emancipating himself and quietly slipping into Boston by the late 1820s. In what may be an apocryphal story (but one that a prominent contemporary journalist swore was based in fact), Cunningham went to extraordinary lengths to earn his freedom.

On that day in 1827, Cunningham's worst fear had been realized: someone from his previous life as an enslaved man had recognized him. One might think that the odds of coming across someone on a crowded city street from years ago and far away would be slim, given the vast territorial reach of the nation and the millions of people who were already making the United States a rising world power. Yet such chance meetings happened all the time in pre–Civil War America. Even as they tried to carve out new lives in free cities, fugitives were constantly fearful of being discovered and returned to bondage. These encounters happened often by accident, when, for example, a traveler from Savannah sitting in a New York coffeehouse suddenly recognized a man or woman who escaped long ago. But such encounters were also frequently deliberate, since slave owners paid agents to surreptitiously travel to free states to recapture runaways. Secret agents of the slave power lurked in the streets, ports, and neighborhoods of every free town and city in the North and West, armed with detailed descriptions of their prey. Slave owners and agents knew that they could count on the help of white police, since the Constitution itself promised in its Fugitive Slave Clause to return the self-emancipated, an agreement between the free and slave states that would be reinforced in laws in 1793 and again in 1850.

So when Seymour Cunningham was confronted by his former master's agent, he knew that the nation's entire political and legal system were arrayed against him. Fortunately, he could count on a few allies. As he was challenged in the street, fellow people of color gathered round to defend him if needed. One of them asked what the fuss was about. The white agent replied: "That villain denies that he is a Slave; and these black rascals are disposed to resist the civil authority, and attempt to rescue him." Together the growing crowd accompanied Cunningham and the agent to the local magistrate's office. There Cunningham denied he was a fugitive, arguing that his freedom papers would prove his free status. All free African Americans, North and South, were required to hold official paper documents indicating their status. Freedom papers were precious documents to free African Americans, for in minute detail they described the physical features of the holder and testified that he or she was not a runaway slave. Cunningham sent a friend to retrieve the papers and return to court. When the papers arrived in the magistrate's hands, the growing crowd of black observers smiled and became confident that they had saved one of their own from being dragged into slavery.

The agent claimed that the free papers were copies of those made for Cunningham's brother, and further he claimed he could prove Seymour was lying. The papers described an individual with a number of physical deformities, most of which had been acquired during the War of 1812. As the agent recounted, the real Seymour Cunningham had a "right arm . . . broken by grape-shot; his little finger of the right hand was shot off; his left leg was broken, and the calf of the other shot away; and he has no middle toe on the right foot." The magistrate then turned to the man in custody, who then raised his right hand to show a missing finger!

Now more furious than ever, the white agent from Virginia claimed that he had just seen the real Seymour Cunningham back in Alexandria, and he promised to return in a few weeks with the authentic Seymour. In the meantime, while the man who claimed to be Seymour was jailed, the real story became public. The brother of the real Seymour Cunningham had indeed copied the original free papers and, realizing that he did not physically conform to the descriptions therein, had gone to a butcher and had paid him to deform his body. At first the butcher, even with the promise of considerable money, refused. "Liberty is sweet," the man steadfastly told the butcher. "I can endure it all, even if you use your cleaver." Cunningham himself had prepared hot tar to be used to stem the bleeding, and when the butcher took off the toe with a mallet it sprang halfway across the room. At each step the butcher worried that if this man died, then he would be charged with murder. But at each hesitation, the soon-to-be Seymour encouraged the butcher to proceed until he had conformed fully to the last detail. Alas, unfortunately for the false Seymour, and despite all of the physical suffering he endured to remain free, he was taken back to bondage in Virginia. Eventually Boston's black and white abolitionists gathered $600 in donations to purchase his freedom.[1]

Although just one man, Seymour Cunningham can tell us much about slavery, the antebellum North, and the coming of the Civil War. Perhaps most obviously, his story reminds us that African Americans' desire for liberty was a potent force in

American politics. In fact, although gruesome, Cunningham's story is not all that surprising, given that we know how desperately enslaved people wished to flee from bondage. It was that desire, that incredible determination to live free, that would make a mockery of white political leaders' attempts to keep the boundary between slavery and freedom intact.

The Cunningham story also tells us that the commonly assumed strict dichotomy between a slave South and a free North was not as rigid or as simple a division as we might think. Much to the frustration of black and white abolitionists, the North's political and legal system, particularly in cities like New York where a pro-South and even proslavery ideology often dominated local politics, was designed to facilitate the return of suspected fugitives. With little more than a quick hearing based on the testimony of one white person, black people in the nominally free states could be whisked away into slavery. Far from being beacons of liberty, northern communities could be treacherous for people of color, whether they were runaways or born free.

In large part because of African American pressure, states became embroiled in legal battles, as well as outright armed conflict, with one another over slavery and freedom, bitterly dividing northern communities and exacerbating sectional tensions. Historian Steven Hahn has noted that scholarship on the coming of the war depicting "the developing conflict between the 'free-labor' North and the 'slave-labor' South . . . no longer comports very well with what we have been learning."[2] Hahn and other historians have called for reexamining the way we characterize the early 1800s and for revisiting our standard understanding of the coming of the Civil War, especially the narrative pitting an unambiguously free North with a distinct South uniquely dominated by a slave power hegemony.

The North's "free soil" could suddenly become the quicksand of bondage, and considerable work remains to be done to understand both the prevalence of kidnapping and its effect on the coming of the Civil War.³ Except for the important and valuable work of Carol Wilson and David Fiske, modern historians have often assumed that abolitionist cries of "kidnappers" were mere hyperbole, rhetoric designed to delegitimize bondage.⁴ But kidnapping was not just an abolitionist rallying cry; in fact white traders lurked in the streets of free-soil towns and prowled farming communities in the countryside in their hunt for potential profits. Abducting free blacks was the informal, extralegal side to the massive legal traffic in bodies, and thousands of African Americans were tricked or involuntarily taken into enslavement, a forced migration that mocked northern claims of free soil and reinforced African American suspicions that they could not find basic protection of their civil rights in either legal cases under the Fugitive Slave Law or in the hidden underworld of kidnapping. African Americans, painfully aware of the widespread nature of kidnapping, pushed white political leaders to include free blacks in national understandings of what it meant to be a citizen with basic civil rights protections.

Kidnapping in the Early Republic

"Hot spots" of kidnapping could be found around complicated borders, such as the area around Virginia, Delaware, Pennsylvania, and Maryland and the confluence of the Ohio and Mississippi Rivers around Indiana, Kentucky, and Ohio. But kidnapping also occurred far away from these hot spots, in small New England communities and in the rural Midwest. No hard numbers exist, but the ubiquity of kidnapping, and the ease with which free African Americans were sold into bondage, shocked contemporaries. "It is believed by many," an editorial in the abolitionist newspaper *The Emancipator* declared, "that the laws of this country, taken in connection with the prejudice against color, and the general apathy that prevails respecting the wrongs or the destiny of the African race, afford greater temptations and facilities for kidnapping, than are found even on the coast of Africa."[5] Indeed, abolitionists became concerned that kidnapping was so common by the 1830s "that familiarity has greatly blunted the sensibilities of the nation with regard to the heinous crime."[6]

During the colonial era, free African Americans occasionally fell victim to kidnapping, but the closing of the Atlantic slave trade after 1809 reshaped the domestic slave economy and created a profitable opening for whites looking to abduct free blacks and sell them into bondage.[7] After 1810, prices for slaves quickly rose, especially when the opening of fertile southwestern territories in Mississippi and Alabama generated a mass forced migration of more than one million bondspeople. The escalating values of slaves led to a new and truculent form of white criminality: entire gangs worked along the poorly watched borders between free and slave soil. Slavers employed a variety of methods to convert free blacks into chattel, including claiming, tricking, and laundering tactics. Shortly after the closing of the foreign slave trade, physician and writer Jesse Torrey toured America and uncovered numerous cases of kidnapping on supposedly free soil. In his widely published travel account, Torrey denounced "the safety with which the free born inhabitants of the United States may be offered for sale and sold, even in the metropolis of Liberty, as oxen; even to those who are notified of the fact, and are perhaps convinced of it, that they are free!"[8] This defining feature of life for northern African Americans fundamentally shaped not only the black experience but the course of national politics as well. As historian Paul Finkelman has argued, state governments struggled with how to protect and police slavery and freedom, resulting in a precarious and ad hoc balance between the needs of bondage and free territories.[9]

The kidnapping of free blacks was rampant in the decades before the Civil War, especially along the thousand-mile border between the free and slave states running from Kansas and Missouri to Pennsylvania and Maryland. Contemporaries estimated that yearly figures in the early 1800s numbered in the hundreds and grew dramatically worse by the 1850s.[10] Alas, once swallowed by the slave trade, few blacks returned to freedom, in large part because traders learned quickly to sell and resell slaves, throwing into shadowy obscurity the background of the kidnapped. Children became the most easily targeted for kidnapping because their facial features and bodies changed so quickly, and because they were easily deceived and cheated into the hands of profiteers and traders. Once kidnapped and laundered into bondage, children—especially the youngest victims—would likely disappear from their families forever.

Two key developments in the early 1800s facilitated the kidnapping of free blacks and simultaneously caused interstate agitation.[11] The transportation revolution of the early 1800s, particularly the increasing use of steamboats and the construction of roads and canals, made kidnapping easier; victims were whisked away on all manner of conveyances. Once enticed into a makeshift storefront or on board a boat, the victim was quickly chained in a basement or below deck to await transportation to slave territory, where the process of laundering free blacks quickly set in. Steamboats were both a common means of escape for runaways and a vehicle for transporting kidnapped free persons of color.[12] For example, eight petitioners from the Gray and Scarborough families argued before a Tennessee judge that kidnappers had taken the "complainants and with force and arms carried them on board of a steamboat," intending to sell them into slavery in Kentucky.[13] A second development in the period frayed relationships between states: the constant disputes over kidnapping were made worse by the antebellum improvements in the postal service and long-distance communication. The telegraph relayed stories of kidnapping almost immediately, and if not sent electronically, information spread within days through letters, newspapers, and magazines circulated nationally by an increasingly sophisticated postal system.[14]

By the 1820s, American cities like Philadelphia and Boston festered with proslavery spies who relied on the collusion of white local officials in the North. As historian James Brewer Stewart has pointed out, racial ideology hardened in this decade, as witnessed by a series of race riots in free cities and by the "new internal divisions of class and culture."[15] The emergence of a modern racist sensibility among whites emerged at the same time that the nation began experiencing the effects of urbanization, industrialization, advances in transportation, the rapid growth of a cotton slave economy in the South, and the prominence of sectional and territorial differences in the wake of the Missouri crisis. Taken together the changing features of life in the 1820s have traditionally marked the beginning of historical constructions like "the age of Jackson" and "the antebellum era," but from the perspective of African Americans, the 1820s mark the beginning of a distinct historical phase that might more properly be called the long Civil War.

That kidnapping emerged as a key issue for African Americans in the 1820s reflected the rise of northern free black populations. By 1838 Philadelphia's pamphlet on "The Present State and Condition of the Free People of Color" reported that nearly 14,000 people of color lived in and around the city, and by 1860 about 225,000 blacks lived in the free states.[16] Whereas a previous generation of scholarship led by historians like Leon Litwack, Leonard Richards, and Gary Nash stressed the gradual, even halting, transition from slavery to freedom in the northern early republic, new work has enshrined cities like Philadelphia as beacons of freedom for runaways.[17] Ira Berlin has memorably argued that early in the nation's history the southern states became "slave societies" and remained that way until the Thirteenth Amendment, while during the colonial era northern states were "societies with slaves," resisting and then by the early 1800s finally rejecting the planter hegemony that came to dominate the South. From the viewpoint of black Americans free and slave, however, this was a distinction with very little difference. While the intense drive for liberty led them north, African Americans knew that only by crossing the Canadian border could they truly find peace.[18]

Several notorious gangs sought prey along the border states, spurred by the crackdown on illegal international slave-trading in the period between 1818 and 1821.[19] With one primary means of importing slaves over the Atlantic and into ports like Baltimore choked off, domestic traders saw another opening. Historian Julie Winch has estimated that by the 1820s forty to sixty African American children were kidnapped each year from Philadelphia alone, despite the valiant efforts of the Pennsylvania Abolition Society (PAS) to thwart the practice. Historian Richard S. Newman found that kidnapping cases in the Philadelphia region numbered in the "hundreds over the space of just a few years and even more still over the course of a decade."[20] Reports of missing children, most of them males between eight and fifteen years old, kept Philadelphia's mayor and local abolitionists busy.[21] The process of laundering African Americans through sale and resale proved highly effective for slave traders. By falsifying "original" purchase receipts, slave catchers and their trading partners could cover their illegal tracks and erase the free past of black northerners, repeatedly sneaking back into free soil to kidnap African Americans.[22]

One of the most notorious bands in the early republic, Patty Cannon's gang, trolled Philadelphia's wharves and neighborhood streets in the 1820s. Contemporaries described Martha Cannon, known as Patty, in racialized terms as "Gypsy-like" in appearance, with dark hair and eyes.[23] Born around 1760, Cannon strategically placed her home on the border between Maryland and Delaware on the Delmarva Peninsula, and as a tavern keeper she often overheard gossip about the domestic slave trade.[24] By the 1820s, when she was in her sixties or seventies, Cannon's role as leader of a kidnapping gang blurred gender norms, and she was described by contemporaries as appearing "more like a man than a woman."[25]

When the Atlantic slave trade mostly shut down after 1809, profiteers anticipated that the domestic supply of bondspeople would rise in value, and Cannon used her family and acquaintances to cash in. Enlisting her son-in-law and several conspirators, Cannon captured scores of free Philadelphians in the 1820s, resulting in an ongoing interstate conflict between Pennsylvania, Maryland, Delaware, Virginia, and Alabama. Among her accomplices was an unscrupulous Philadelphia African American named Henry Carr, who allowed Joseph Johnson to use his storefront as a place to hold kidnapped young boys. Cannon owned land in Alabama and her son-in-law transported victims by boat.[26]

When caught, as she and her conspirators were in the early 1820s, Cannon often bribed local sheriffs to look the other way. Philadelphia mayor Joseph Watson, however, refused to ignore the constant complaints from black residents that men, women, and children were disappearing at alarming rates, and the mayor himself resented the embarrassing pilfering of local citizens. Working with the PAS, Watson wrote letters and dispatched representatives to southern states, happily reporting to the city council in 1828 that nearly a dozen victims had been recovered.[27] However, much to Watson's dismay, Philadelphia's police seemed indifferent to the kidnappings, and the complicity of local officials meant that Cannon and her gang operated almost with impunity.[28] It seemed to matter little whether African Americans held documents demonstrating their free status or not. Philadelphia had already witnessed the first of several ongoing antiblack and antiabolition riots, and local politicians and legal authorities worried that protecting African Americans would cost them white support.[29] Interestingly, white southerners sometimes notified northern authorities of suspicious slave transactions. Watson endeavored to remain vigilant, succeeding in recovering kidnapped residents like Samuel Scomp, who had been lured aboard a boat by the promise of being paid to unload a stock of produce.[30]

Scomp had been just one of the scores of those kidnapped by the Cannon Gang, whose network stretched across several states, and only when Cannon herself was accused of murder was she finally brought to justice. A Maryland farmer working on Cannon's land discovered dead bodies in a chest; hidden inside were the corpses of a black woman and her baby, as well as the bones of others.[31] White authorities could not ignore these accusations, and local officials in Delaware brought murder charges against Cannon. Salacious newspaper accounts dramatically recounted the treacherous acts of America's first female serial killer, and the press would circulate a pamphlet detailing her crimes.[32] Cannon spent several months in jail, until she apparently committed suicide in 1829, but not before causing a fierce interstate conflict over kidnapping and the meaning of free soil that prefigured the battles of the Civil War.[33]

In the case of the Cannon Gang, Philadelphia mayor Joseph Watson demonstrated that some northern public officials worked hard to recover black victims of kidnapping, but many more authorities, from northern police to profiteers, had every interest in ignoring kidnapping or even participating actively in the process. Of this northern African Americans themselves were keenly aware. They sought redress in northern courts, as the many petitions for freedom in state and federal courts attest. However, in petitioning the courts, free blacks were forced to recognize "the idea of *just* subjection under slave law."[34] Kidnapped African Americans had little choice but to acknowledge the legitimacy of legal claims to runaways by proclaiming themselves not to be fugitives but victims of abduction. In 1827, the same year that Seymour Cunningham disfigured his body to comport with free papers, John Singleton claimed that he was born to a free woman of color in Illinois. He fell victim to kidnapping by a white criminal named Jeptha Lamkins, who dragged him into slavery in Alabama. Lamkins then quickly sold Singleton; Singleton sued his new master for his freedom but then was sold to a trader in New Orleans before the case was decided. Remarkably, Singleton escaped from bondage in New Orleans, snuck onto a Mississippi steamboat, and finally landed in St. Louis, where he was arrested and held as a runaway slave![35] Singleton had no recourse but to sue in the county court in St. Louis, having become the object of a domestic slave trade system that relied on the quick selling and reselling of a free person of color to obliterate his or her past.

Such "laundering" of free black people was a common enough practice that African Americans feared being permanently lost in bondage. For example, Ralph was a free person of color hired by Missouri merchants who then tried to enslave him by falsifying bills of sale designed to counteract his freedom papers. Ironically, in using the legal system to proclaim their status as free blacks, victims of kidnapping legitimized the Fugitive Slave Law. Their cases hinged precariously on the existence of freedom papers, formal legal documents with the imprimatur of white judges. Without these papers, which could be easily lost, stolen, or destroyed, and without the ability to

The Long Civil War 25

call black witnesses, kidnapped blacks faced steep hurdles to prove their free status. Before the Third Judicial Circuit of Missouri, Ralph sued the merchants, expressing his fear by saying, "It is the intention of said James & Coleman to take your petitioner to some place where the fact of his freedom is unknown & sell him for a slave."[36] Such concern was entirely warranted. Joseph Bedney, a teenager of mixed race parentage, claimed that he was born free and then hired as a waiter in Ohio in 1838. Bedney's duplicitous Ohio master took advantage of the apprenticeship and sold Bedney to a Missouri slave trader, who took him to Texas, where he was sold again to an Alabama dealer, who in turn put him up for auction in New Orleans. He sued in the First Judicial District Court in Orleans Parish, stating unequivocally his fear that if he were sold yet again, he would be "deprived of ever again asserting his freedom."[37] Fortunately for Bedney, Judge A. M. Buchanan agreed with Bedney and granted the petition. Free persons of color like Bedney knew that once they were removed from their local surroundings, the possibility of remaining free diminished dramatically, and they repeatedly petitioned courts to keep them within state borders.[38]

Alas, a favorable outcome in a given case did not by any means ensure that freedom was permanently guaranteed. On the contrary, even after proving their free status in court, African Americans could find themselves in danger again of being turned into chattel property within years or even months. John Merry faced such circumstances twice in the 1820s, once in Missouri and again in Louisiana, and Jones H. Jenkins had to prove his free status twice in the 1830s.[39] Similarly, Caroline, a young free person of color born to a white mother and black father, sued in Kentucky courts for protection. Her mother had placed her in the hands of an "unnatural and inhuman uncle," who sold her to traders, who then "detained her as a slave" in Louisville.[40] Though young, Caroline knew that if she were taken out of Kentucky, her chances of proving her free status would reach another level of difficulty.

The increasingly porous nature of the borders between slavery and freedom, easier to cross with the construction of each new road, railroad, port, and canal, had significant implications for the nation's crisis over slavery. Self-emancipated men and women fled bondage to search for freedom in the free states or in Canada, hotly pursued by professional slave catchers venturing north in search of runaways who could be returned for reward money. Slave stealers descended on plantations, whisked away the enslaved, and resold them in neighboring states or in faraway southwestern lands. Kidnappers snuck into free communities, abducted African Americans whether they were born free or enslaved, and sold them into bondage.

The problem had become so acute in the eyes of slaveholders by the 1830s that rescuing bondspeople became a thorny issue between free and slave states. Governors, legislators, and other state and local officials argued vehemently across the country, charging each other with violating the Constitution and long-established rules of comity. In one such interstate incident, a fugitive had secreted himself in the hold of a ship in Savannah that was bound for Maine. Weary and frustrated by the constant flow of runaways, and the role of northern ships in helping them to escape, the slave owners followed the ship all the way up the coast to Maine. Georgia's governor submitted an extradition request that was ignored by his counterpart in Maine. State legislators in South Carolina, in support of their Georgia neighbors, passed a series of resolutions charging the free states with a "failure" to fulfill their "constitutional obligations" to return not just the self-emancipated but those who abetted escapes. Such intransigence, South Carolinians declared, "will be a fatal blow to the security of our institutions and property."[41] Yet, the hotly disputed cases over kidnappings and runaways continued between state governments throughout the 1830s.

In an article titled "Another Inter-state War Impending," one abolitionist paper highlighted the legal and political battles waged between state capitols, even as Washington politicians tried to ignore or smooth over the problems over slavery. In fact, abolitionists believed "that the readers of the political papers are kept in the dark as to the causes that are in operation to disturb the public tranquility and shake the union of these states."[42] Political leaders of both parties sought to maintain the carefully drawn lines between freedom and slavery, but every day the actions of Americans themselves erased those lines.

The legal and illegal abduction of African Americans shaped the national debate over freedom and slavery in fundamental ways. In the legal battles between free and slave states, the fight over free blacks working as seamen on trading ships became one of the most contentious issues.[43] Southern states, worried about the potential for free black sailors to promote slave insurrections or escapes, passed Negro Seamen Acts requiring the jailing of any crewmen stationed overnight. Edlie Wong, who has studied the laws and their implications for blurring the lines between freedom and slavery, particularly in regard to freedom of travel, points out that the laws caused considerable friction between North and South, beginning, significantly, in the early 1820s. South Carolina passed its Negro Seamen Act in 1822 in the wake of Denmark Vesey's plot to incite an insurrection. Yet, as Wong points out, white southerners toughened the laws throughout the 1820s and 1830s, stiffening punishments and even threatening to sell free black mariners as slaves.[44] Northern states pleaded with courts to consider the constitutionality of the Negro Seamen Acts, but southerners successfully thwarted attempts to hear cases in federal courts. African Americans and their white antislavery allies viewed the laws as little more than legalized kidnapping. As one reformer put it, the laws amounted to "the *State* trying to reduce human beings from a state of freedom into that of slavery."[45] Northern merchants, upset by the disruption in trade the imprisonments caused, petitioned federal lawmakers to nullify southern laws.[46] African Americans themselves forced northern shippers to acknowledge the severity of the problem. Worried that they would be kidnapped and sold into slavery through southern seamen's laws, eighteen black mariners staged a mutiny on a ship when they found out they would be heading to Mobile.[47] According to one contemporary estimate, well over one thousand free black sailors from New York alone were jailed and sold as slaves *each year* at the height of the practice around 1850.[48]

Freedom of travel and trade had been severely curtailed for African American sailors and by extension for their northern employers, and the issue became, in the words of one contemporary, the thorniest issue in maintaining good relations between the sections "since the formation of the government."[49] Just how acutely the issue damaged the Union became clear in 1844 when Massachusetts sent one of its most esteemed lawyers, Samuel Hoar, to Charleston to plead its case. South Carolina's legislators, however, caught wind of the visit and authorized their governor to throw him out as an "emissary of a Foreign Government, hostile to our Democratic Institutions, and with the sole purpose of subverting our internal police."[50] While the state authorities escorted Hoar out of the city before he was lynched, papers across the country recounted how the interstate dispute reflected the deepening chasm within the Union. Similar conflicts between Virginia and New York, and Georgia and New York, over kidnappings and attempts to recapture the self-emancipated in the 1840s developed into what increasingly appeared to be a dramatic clash between states that could have no other outcome than civil war.[51]

States routinely accused one another of illegal and unconstitutional activity, from encouraging and harboring kidnappers to facilitating slave escapes. A complex series of legal and extralegal actions kept lawyers, legislators, and judges active, especially in hot spots like the borders between Pennsylvania, Delaware, New Jersey, and Maryland and between Ohio, Kentucky, Missouri, and Virginia.[52] South-Central Pennsylvania and the land on either side of the Ohio River between Kentucky and Ohio witnessed intense battles as blacks and whites, free people and slaves, hunters and victims crossed and recrossed state borders to fight over the meaning of freedom and citizenship.[53] The porous nature of these state borders made them difficult to police, and when state constitutions sought to prohibit slavery within their boundaries, free states became increasingly frustrated that they might as well not have borders at all. Indiana governor Jonathan Jennings complained that the neighboring slave state of Kentucky repeatedly violated the border and established fugitive rendition laws that made a mockery of Indiana's attempt to remain free soil. Laws making kidnapping easier, Jennings complained, were "calculated to impair the rights of the sovereignty of the state."[54]

One of the earliest and most remarkable examples of collective action on the part of African Americans occurred in Boston in the summer of 1836, an incident that seems to have laid the groundwork for similar rescue attempts in Boston and across the nation throughout the antebellum era. The Boston incident was precipitated by the actions of two Baltimore women, Anna Patten and Eliza Small, who ran away from their Baltimore master in late July 1836. Fleeing under pseudonyms, they managed to acquire (presumably falsified) free papers and boarded a ship for Boston as free women. Almost immediately, their owner hired a Baltimore police officer, Mathew Turner, to go to Boston, armed with power of attorney, and seize the fugitives. Turner managed to get the ship's captain to hold the women on board while Turner went to secure a warrant for the women's arrest.

Somehow, Boston's black community, always ready to spring into action when needed, heard about the impending arrests and gathered by the dozens along the docks and in boats. With the help of African American community leader S. H. Adams, they secured a writ of habeas corpus and took Anna and Eliza away from the wharf. At first the women were afraid that they were being arrested on the ship, but when they discovered the writ had been issued, one cried out that "she knew God would not forsake her and leave her to be sent back to the South." Prominent Boston abolitionist attorney Samuel E. Sewall pledged to represent Patten and Small in court, but Boston's African Americans, wary of the legitimacy of the process, determined to keep a careful watch on the proceedings, ready to take action if necessary.[55]

Unlike the cases of other fugitives, this time Boston's legal system favored Anna and Eliza. On the day of their hearing in the Massachusetts Supreme Judicial Court in early August 1836, the court was crowded with African Americans, especially women. With Judge Lemuel Shaw presiding, Turner was immediately put on the defensive when he had to ask for more time to gather evidence that the two women belonged to Baltimore slave owner John B. Morris. Shaw replied testily that the women had already been imprisoned for several days and that evidence should have been secured well beforehand. Shaw rendered a short decision that neither Turner nor the ship's captain had the right to detain the women and was ready to discharge the women when Turner rose before the court and yelled out, "Discharged or not discharged, I shall detain them."[56]

Almost immediately the court erupted. African Americans outside the court, either listening in to the closed proceedings or receiving a signal from those inside, began to push the courtroom doors open, even as Judge Shaw himself ran from the bench to buttress those keeping the door shut. Shaw and the court officials were quickly overwhelmed, and African Americans flooded into the court. Aided by the considerable crowd inside the room, they brought the women downstairs and outside to a waiting coach.[57] As Patten and Small headed into the coach, "a number of black women divested themselves of shawls, bonnets, etc. and offered them to the slaves, after which the carriage drove off, followed by the crowd, consisting of four or five hundred blacks of all ages and both sexes, shouting 'hurrah for freedom.'"[58] A flustered Judge Shaw ordered the women back into the court so that they could be officially discharged, but it was too late. Sewall apologized for the disruption, but a white female abolitionist stood up and lectured Constable Turner as Shaw adjourned the court.[59] The rescue was unprecedented.[60]

The women were never recaptured, but the case of Anna Patten and Eliza Small provided lasting lessons to Bostonians. The city's African Americans from then on stood ready to rescue accused runaways, and collective action in the form of mobbing courthouses became a pattern repeated not only in Boston but in other northern and midwestern cities as well. Mobbing became one of the most effective tools African Americans could use to thwart renditions and subvert the legal process.

White Bostonians, including many opposed to slavery, reacted angrily at the rescue, preferring to let the formal legal proceedings unfold. The *Boston Recorder* and *Boston Transcript* denounced the rescue as "one of the first triumphant entries of Judge Lynch into our city," and other papers decried the validity of the rescue.[61] White abolitionists generally did not approve of the rescue, and even William Lloyd Garrison pointed out that "resistance to the legal authorities we never hesitate to disapprove." Garrison, however, unlike most whites, directed readers' attention to the hypocrisy of the constant harassing and threatening of abolitionists by racial conservatives, the same commenters now condemning Boston's black community for its lawlessness.[62] Judge Shaw would later become a defender of the right of southerners to recover fugitives, while Sewall earned his stripes as a defender of the self-emancipated. But slave societies throughout the New World took notice of the mob action as well. Virginia's *Alexandria Gazette* featured two stories on the rescue, and Trinidad's *Port of Spain Gazette* reprinted a lengthy report of the extralegal action.[63]

Despite the unease of white Bostonians, black Americans realized that with the entirety of the political and legal system arrayed against them, extralegal methods like mobbing courthouses were perfectly legitimate ways to defend basic human rights. Even as the fugitive crises divided cities like Boston, they simultaneously drove sharp wedges into relationships between states. In July 1839, a slave sought shelter on a Virginia ship bound for New York, apparently with the consent of the captain. The indignant governor of Virginia, David Campbell, referenced the dispute between Maine and Georgia as he spoke to the legislature on the controversy between Virginia and New York. William Henry Seward, governor of New York, had refused to extradite the men who had helped the slave escape because he did not consider the matter to fall within the constitutional demand to return anyone suspected of "treason, felony, or other crime." Seward was denying that simply helping to transport a slave who wished to emancipate himself was a crime. An incredulous Campbell denounced Seward for ignoring his "plain and manifest constitutional duty," a serious charge that reflected the heated nature of the interstate dispute. "If the Governor of New York is right," Campbell declared, "he is bound not only to protect those who steal our slaves, but those who incite and assist them to abscond from their masters." Campbell argued, with some justification, that Seward's interpretation of the Constitution represented a fundamental shift in the interstate comity that had governed relations between state governments since ratification. With this shift in northern thinking, Campbell charged, "It is impossible that the Union can continue long."[64]

Borders, Kidnapping, and Runaways in the West

While historians have focused on the Mason-Dixon Line separating bondage and freedom in the East, increasingly scholars are examining the borders farther west. The Ohio River valley between the slave state of Kentucky and the free states of Indiana and Ohio witnessed intense battles over slavery, particularly as internal improvements greatly enhanced mobility. The movement of white and black Americans was made much easier by their proximity to major river systems, and the Mississippi River in particular witnessed advances in the speed, affordability, and safety of travel by steamboat.

Historians like Matthew Salafia and Christopher Phillips have revealed a world that was far removed ideologically and geographically from the sectional debates farther east. Washington political leaders were determined to maintain the slavery divide; in fact, as became crystal clear by the Missouri Crisis in 1819–20, the future of the Union depended on defending that divide. But as Salafia points out in his study of the antebellum Ohio River valley, whites profited markedly from a border that was porous. In fact, Salafia argues that there were not two different societies north and south of the river; rather, a regional society and economy countenanced the constant cross-river movement of people (even enslaved people) because such mobility allowed whites to hire black laborers without asking about their free or slave status. White merchants north of the Ohio River could hire cheap labor without reference to status, blurring contemporary attempts to draw sharp lines between free and slave labor. The river, he demonstrates, "was a place where confrontation coexisted with accommodation."[65] The West defies our conventional bifurcated understanding of slavery's divide, a point demonstrated by the fact that Unionism prevailed in the minds of Ohio River valley residents even as the nation was literally separating during secession. Historian Christopher Phillips rightly cautions us that "any application of a 'One North' model to states lying above the western rivers" is deeply problematic.[66] Along with scholars who have studied the Middle Border region such as Anne Marshall and Aaron Astor, Salafia and Phillips remind us that the western territories created their own political culture, a culture that certainly overlapped with the national debates over slavery and free soil but that was also shaped by local circumstances, including the benefits of maintaining a contingent, rather than a hardened, separation.[67]

Yet, even as such deliberate ambiguity between different labor systems enriched white farmers and merchants, it simultaneously opened a space for illicit activities, and once again kidnappers stepped into that space to capture people of color and sell them as slaves. The kidnapping of free African Americans in the West was every bit as brutal as in the East, and local newspapers harbor tales of innumerable abductions. In Indiana on September 1, 1836, a gang of five whites from Posey County approached the home of "an industrious negro" and his family near Evansville. Situated on the Ohio River near the Wabash River, Evansville witnessed a rash of kidnappings in the 1830s and 1840s. Late in the evening they knocked and claimed that they wanted to hire the father to chop wood, but he knew that kidnappers prowled the area and refused to go with the men, pulling his rifle from the wall above his bed in hopes of warding off the bandits. Before he could fire, however, the men knocked him down, breaking his breastbone, and seized him and his family. Within a short time, the family had been snatched away to Mount Vernon, further along the Ohio River, and locked away on a ferry bound for the South. The father, despite his painful state, escaped to get help, but when he returned, his family had already been sold into slavery, while the kidnappers had escaped the law.[68]

Such heartbreaking stories were repeated in western papers throughout the late antebellum era and were picked up by abolitionist papers in the East. New York's *The Emancipator* dutifully reported the news of western outrages, including a single article's account, in the summer of 1838, of three kidnapping cases. The first involved Samuel Devall, an African American "whose parents [were] worthy and respectable citizens of Pittsburgh." Boarding the steamer *London* in Cincinnati to visit his parents in Pittsburgh, Devall was confronted by a Captain Patterson, who demanded to see Devall's free papers. Being born free, Devall did not have such documentation with him, and Patterson succeeded in having Devall jailed in Cincinnati until he could prove his free status. Devall's distraught parents rushed to provide documents testifying to his status, and he was eventually liberated from jail.

The second case announced in *The Emancipator* also involved a young African American and distraught parents who refused to acquiesce to an injustice. In April 1838, the mother of eighteen-year-old Isaac Cohen desperately sought help from legal offices in Louisville. Her son had left their home in Bethlehem, Iowa, and attempted to travel by steamboat to Louisville, when a Kentucky postmaster named Asa Abbott arrested and jailed him for supposedly being a runaway. Like Devall, Cohen did not have free papers and so was subject to being sold into slavery.

The final case returned the reader's focus back to kidnapping in Ohio, telling the story of John Burns, a Maryland slave owner who migrated to Ohio with his slaves in tow. The bondspeople were unaware at first that slavery was illegal in

Ohio, but when one of the enslaved men caught wind of this fact, he confronted Burns and refused to work, walking away from Burns's farm determined to make his own way as a free man. Burns succeeded in hiring two men to track him down, tie him up, and sell him into permanent bondage farther south.

For *The Emancipator* and its New York editor Charles Dennison, the stories of African Americans fighting back against kidnapping and a corrupt legal system that jailed freeborn men were inspiring, even if they had taken place out west. But the newspaper, like many abolitionist outlets, was not above a bit of moralizing and patronizing of its own. In particular, the paper pointed out that all the recent stories of kidnapping had taken place on or near rivers, which had made the swift abductions easier. "We have a suggestion to make to our colored friends," an editorial in the paper warned. "You see the dangers to which you are exposed in steamboat and river-business: why will you not avoid them?" The paper, obviously engaged in blaming the victims, particularly admonished black parents to keep their children "away from the *river*." And yet the paper might as well have blamed the rivers themselves, or the invention of steamboats and their widespread usage for travel, or the transportation revolution that was transforming the nation and each day making it easier for black bodies to be moved, abducted, or jailed.[69] Combined with the powerful desire of African Americans for freedom, modernization—the dizzying rate of industrialization and urbanization—was pressuring the system and its unsustainable boundaries between slavery and freedom.

In abducting free blacks, kidnappers assumed great risks, and over time they learned creative ways to trick African Americans into enslavement. White police, constables, and abductors posing as officials realized that approaching someone with charges of being a fugitive slave would cause the accused to lash out in violence, run for her or his life, or scream aloud to alert fellow African Americans. So rather than immediately charge an African American with being a runaway, kidnappers and their official accomplices often arrested blacks for some petty crime. Slave catchers and their associates lied to the accused, revealing only later the true nature of the arrest. William Still, an important black conductor on the Underground Railroad, recalled the case of Henry Tiffin, a Philadelphia African American arrested as a runaway. At first the sheriff seized Tiffin under the charge of petty theft, but Tiffin was soon accused of being Michael Brown, an escaped Baltimore slave.[70]

"Claiming" a free African American as runaway property, another form of kidnapping with the imprimatur of legality, became commonplace in the antebellum period. Slave traders and putative owners counted on white northern judges, sheriffs, justices of the peace, and town constables to return accused runaways, often with little more than a bill of sale and white testimony. Free-soil states commonly prohibited black testimony in court, so African Americans known to their black neighbors for many years could not call such witnesses to testify on their behalf. Claiming a slave became a safer form of kidnapping, one that relied not on guns and violent coercion but instead on a swift legal proceeding. The result was the same. Free blacks could be claimed on free soil and taken into bondage.

Cases of dishonest whites falsely laying claim to free blacks can be found throughout the antebellum era, in all corners of the Midwest and Northeast. Martin Mitchell claimed in a Missouri court in 1832 that he owned Mahala, a free black born in Illinois. Mahala in turn asked the court to grant her counsel as a poor person, and specifically to prevent Mitchell from taking her into a slave state before she could establish her freedom.[71] Doing so depended on freedom papers, usually little more than one-page documents containing descriptions of bearers and white testimony as to their free status. Absent these documents, blacks faced steep hurdles in proving their standing as free persons. For Mahala, the assumption was that she was a runaway until she could prove otherwise, and she was held in a St. Louis jail until the hearing. Similarly, William Richardson claimed he was born in Canada but was confined to a jail in Washington, D.C., as a runaway.[72] An African American named Comfort maintained that Thomas Smith illegally held her as a slave, and she requested that a Delaware court summon Smith and recognize her freedom.[73]

Many falsely claimed or kidnapped blacks like Mahala and Comfort had been tricked into bondage. Scholars have long recognized trickster tales as fundamental tropes in black American culture, presuming that such tales originated in African societies, were imported during the Middle Passage, and were mixed with southern U.S. and Caribbean stories.[74] But such tales also undoubtedly doubled as cautionary tales to keep African Americans—especially children—from falling prey to duplicitous whites and their black allies. In Kate E. R. Pickard's novel *The Kidnapped and the Ransomed*, black children are tricked into slavery in Kentucky. There they are told to make a life with their new "mother," but the abducted boys dramatically scream, "No! No! . . . that's not our mother!"[75] Trickery leading to kidnapping could result from the promise of payment for work, an agreement to arrange transportation, or the hope of seeing a loved one. Poor and unemployed blacks also fell victim to "traps set by kidnappers who advertised jobs."[76] Such kidnappers also took advantage of high illiteracy, tricking people into signing documents to their detriment, or employing deceitful tactics to trick well-meaning whites. Lydia Cooper had been manumitted in the early 1800s by her master John Cooper, after which she moved to Maryland, married, and had three children. Some twenty years later, however, a relative of the original owner tricked John Cooper into believing that the manumissions were invalid, and John signed over title of the former slaves to the relative, who then tried to sell the woman and her family into slavery even though she had been free for more than two decades.[77]

As women like Cooper sought help in the courts, they pressed the legal and political system to protect their free status. Neither system, however, proved equal to the task. Ohio, Pennsylvania, Indiana, and other free states enacted legislation to limit the political influence of African Americans, even as they simultaneously passed personal liberty laws to prevent slave catchers and kidnappers from seizing their black citizens.[78] For example, Ohio passed a Fugitive Slave Law in 1839 to facilitate the return of runaways, a reflection of the conservative racial opinions of its white citizens. Historians have found that, throughout the antebellum era, most Ohio residents remained hostile to the settling of black runaways in their towns and suspicious of abolitionists. Ohio's law to prevent runaways passed upon a request from Kentucky slaveholders, who resented the crossing of their "property" across the Ohio River. So eager were Ohio's political leaders to accommodate southern planters that the state house of representatives passed the new Fugitive Slave Law by fifty-four to thirteen.[79] Such a lopsided tally obscured the fact that white Ohioans remained deeply divided over the meanings of slavery and freedom. As Jonathan Earle has pointed out, Cincinnati harbored a schism between pro- and antislavery forces, while the Western Reserve, a region settled mostly by transplanted Yankees, remained reliably antislavery and pro-Whig.[80] Antiabolition mobs erupted in northern cities like Philadelphia, New York, Cincinnati, and Boston throughout the early 1800s.

For their part, African Americans greatly resented white northerners' complicity in returning runaways and the blind eye they turned to kidnapping, and they constantly reminded white politicians of the need to expand the meanings of freedom and citizenship to include free blacks. As soon as kidnapping became a grave concern, African Americans mobilized to protect their brothers and sisters and to make white political leaders aware of the problem. In 1819 Baltimore's black community established a relief society and a few years later founded the Society for the Protection of Free People of Color.[81] In fact, Maryland's African Americans maintained watch patrols specifically to thwart kidnappings.[82]

The antislavery press also continued to sound the alarm, demanding that white northern officials ignore southern calls for their help in gathering victims. In the newspaper *Freedom's Journal*, John Brown Russwurm decried "the business of arresting our brethren as runaways" whether they were former slaves or not.[83] Jermain Wesley Loguen, a black abolitionist in New York, complained to Governor Washington Hunt of "the fiendish machinations of the merciless slave-hunter, and their equally guilty, but infinitely meaner more contemptible Northern abettors (officials and non-officials)."[84] Black leaders like Russwurm and Loguen worked tirelessly against white complacency, refusing to countenance comments from their purported allies. For example, James McCune Smith, a black physician and abolitionist, repudiated William Henry Seward for using "an expression about 'inferiority of race' which I can forgive in no man."[85] Smith pushed white abolitionists to reject Seward's racism, even complaining to his friend Gerrit Smith (a prominent white abolitionist) that white antislavery activists should not reject just bondage but racism as well. In a letter to prominent black abolitionist William C. Nell, William Anderson attacked Horace Greeley for racist rhetoric during a political campaign.[86] Embarrassed into action by African Americans, white free-soil political leaders responded to violations of their borders by charging slave catchers with kidnapping.[87]

Northern blacks realized the contested nature of their freedom, cognizant that they were only "half-free," ever-attuned to the "man stealers" who might turn them into slaves and wary of those who appeared too friendly or overly interested in their pasts.[88] As self-emancipated Pennsylvanian William Parker put it, "After a few years of life in a Free State, I found by bitter experience that to preserve my stolen liberty I must pay, unremittingly, an almost sleepless vigilance."[89] Such vigilance found expression in armed resistance, but it also emerged in intellectual, cultural, and political ways as African Americans fought to reformulate definitions of citizenship and freedom. The constant push to end kidnapping, to get white political leaders to see that literally thousands of free blacks who had never been slaves had fallen victim to abduction, remains one of the most significant and underappreciated movements in the long struggle over civil rights in America, reminding us of the precarious nature of liberty for northern black Americans while also helping to explain the urgency of African Americans and their allies in the sectional crisis.[90] Examining the two sides of abduction—illegal kidnapping and legalized seizures under the Fugitive Slave Law—helps us to understand the coming of the Civil War by highlighting black activism as well as the division within the antebellum North over the issue of abduction. The perspective of African American history makes clear that civil conflicts over race, the meaning of state borders, and basic civil rights protections against abduction had deep roots in the early republic, roots that extend our chronological understanding of the coming of the Civil War. In a crisis already apparent in the 1820s, kidnapping and the porous nature of borders between free and slave territories set in motion tensions that would lead to disunion.

CHAPTER TWO

The Making of the Fugitive Slave Law and the Sectional Crisis

Central to the story of the free states, slavery, and the coming of the Civil War is the tremendous fury expressed by black and white northerners and westerners in the wake of the Fugitive Slave Law of 1850. The anger over the Fugitive Slave Law was not just one factor among many that led to civil war but was in fact fundamental in shaping the course of sectional hostility in two key ways. The law caused a dramatic shift in black and white opinion on the feasibility of compromise. Among many northern whites, the Compromise of 1850 and especially the Fugitive Slave Law weakened the Second Party System by significantly sharpening voter mistrust of national political leaders and their parties and rendering even talk of compromise anathema among northerners. African American reaction to the law sparked a flee-or-fight response; those who saw no hope for African Americans in the nation after the Fugitive Slave Law pursued emigration with renewed zeal, while those determined to remain in the country and fight white racism and attempts to capture runaways pledged a new commitment to combating state and federal laws with armed resistance.

A powerful succession of action and reaction developed in the wake of the law, in which suspected runaways were captured by northern authorities, freed by angry biracial mobs, and followed by the inevitable eruption of white southern indignation at northern refusal to follow the Constitution and federal laws. Northern reaction to enforcing the Fugitive Slave Law convinced even moderate white southerners that compromise with the North would be impossible. And moderate white northerners could no longer claim with credibility that slavery was merely a southern problem and of little concern to northern citizens.[1] At the same time and in similar ways, the cycle of action and reaction diminished the ability of moderates in each section to make the case for the feasibility of compromise over slavery.

One manifestation of this ideological hardening can be seen in both sections in the development of vigilance committees. Just as northern abolitionists formed vigilance committees in Philadelphia, Boston, and New York to warn of kidnappers and slave catchers in their midst, so too did white southerners form their own vigilance committees to sound the alarm on antislavery activities, especially slave stealing. In fact, as Stanley Harrold contends, "semimilitary organizations, such as slave patrols, sheriff's posses, urban police, and vigilante associations" were ubiquitous in the South.[2] Whites were convinced that abolitionist spies were lurking, alien-like, all around them, and when given the chance these thieves would guide slave property to freedom. In South Carolina, the Spartanburg Committee of Vigilance and Safety kept a watchful eye out for antislavery actions by whites or blacks.[3] A similar organization kept watch in Tuscaloosa.[4] The border states were particularly rife with these kinds of informal armies, and in slave states like Kentucky, Missouri, and Maryland, states from which slaves could more easily run away to free soil, the press and political leaders kept a wary eye on the border. Delia Webster, for example, a New England teacher charged with helping slaves escape from Kentucky, was tried and convicted and became an infamous case of northern perfidy in the eyes of southerners.[5]

So by the 1840s, free African Americans and their white allies in the northern Whig Party were coming to the conclusion that local liberty laws were needed to protect the free states from the reach of slavery. They believed that proper respect for state authority to keep slavery outside their borders abrogated the South's desire to recapture runaways. Northerners and midwesterners began to articulate a legal and political defense of states' rights that legitimated state liberty laws. At the same time, white southerners had become convinced that a new federal law to supersede local and state antislavery statutes was absolutely necessary to keep the Union together. The Fugitive Slave Law, intended to assuage these southerners, ended up pleasing almost no one.

The Latimer Case

George Latimer entered the world like many enslaved peoples, the child of an illicit relationship between a white artisan and a bondswoman. Even as a child, though, Latimer thought frequently about emancipating himself: "I have frequently rolled up my sleeve," Latimer would later remember, "and asked— 'Can this flesh belong to any man as horses do?'" Numerous contemporary observers noticed that Latimer was so light skinned that he could easily pass for a white man, so Latimer used this to his advantage in plotting his escape.[6] Posing as white, and with his wife Rebecca posing as his slave, the couple boarded a ship in Baltimore in early October 1842. Not wishing to be identified on board, the Latimers hid "under the forepeak of the vessel . . . lying on stone ballast in the darkness for nine weary hours." The ship stopped in Philadelphia, and the Latimers arrived in Boston on October 7.

Meanwhile, Latimer's owner, James Gray, posted an ad declaring Latimer "my Negro Man George," describing him as "about 5 feet 3 or 4 inches high, about 22 years of age, his complexion a bright yellow . . . [and] rather silent and slow spoken." Latimer knew Gray's tenaciousness all too well and no doubt suspected that the Virginians would pursue them. As he looked for work among the wharves of Boston harbor, Latimer's luck ran out. He was immediately recognized by William Carpenter, a former resident of Norfolk who had run a rum shop there. Carpenter informed fellow storekeeper James Gray that Latimer had fled to Boston. Given Gray's aggressive nature, Latimer was not surprised when the Virginia storekeeper traveled to Boston to claim his "property" under the Fugitive Slave Clause of the Constitution and the 1793 act supporting it.

Almost immediately Boston lay in turmoil. Newspapers declared that the city was "waiting in breathless anxiety" for the hearing before the Massachusetts Supreme Judicial Court, led by Chief Justice Lemuel Shaw, on the evening of October 20, just a day after Gray had identified Latimer as a fugitive. Shaw and his colleagues deliberated just fifteen minutes before delivering their opinion that enough evidence had been presented to keep Latimer in the city jail.

Beacon Hill's African American community erupted in anger and pledged to rescue Latimer by overtaking the jail, lacking any confidence in the formal legal proceedings. *The Liberator* reported that "immense crowds" of African Americans "thronged around the Court House, in a very feverish state of anxiety."[7] "It seems impossible," announced the abolitionist *Emancipator and Republican*, "that Gray and Latimer should go out of the city together, *both* alive."[8] Black Bostonians planned to use overwhelming numbers to rescue Latimer, employing a strategy of collective action that would become a hallmark of African American resistance.

Boston already had a vibrant, active community of black voices that fought against slavery and racism. William C. Nell, a Boston native, had become active in abolitionism in the

1820s, organizing the Massachusetts General Colored Association and later writing for antislavery newspapers. Nell would ultimately earn fame as a vigorous opponent of segregation and racism, especially in Boston's public schools, but when Latimer was arrested in 1842, Nell was still forming the networks among fellow black activists like Charles L. Remond, perhaps the best-known African American abolitionist in Boston.[9] Remond had traveled with Garrison to the antislavery convention in London in 1840 as a Massachusetts delegate and had spoken before numerous audiences at home and abroad. Thanks to energetic activists like Nell and Remond, Boston's black community mobilized with great alacrity in opposing Latimer's arrest, beginning with a mass meeting at the Belknap Street Church just days after Latimer was jailed.

As Boston's black community mobilized quickly, white antislavery activists maintained their faith in the legal process and refrained from joining black street protests. Instead, they gathered for a rousing meeting at Boston's Faneuil Hall at the end of October to rally in support of the legal doctrine that we usually associate with the Old South: states' rights. Just as the Latimer case proved crucial for African Americans in the development of a strategy of collective action, so too did the case lead to the formation of a northern states' rights ideology redolent of the nullification doctrines articulated in South Carolina a decade earlier. On Sunday evening, October 30, while Latimer remained in Leverett Street Jail, Sewall, Joshua Leavitt, Henry Bowditch, Francis Jackson, and other leading white activists took the podium before a crowd of several hundred to argue that Massachusetts had the right to ignore the Fugitive Slave Clause of the Constitution as well as the 1793 federal act. Sewall declared in Faneuil Hall, "Massachusetts is, and of right ought to be, a free and independent State [and] cannot allow her soil to be polluted by the foot-print of slavery, without trampling on her bill of rights."[10] In response to

Sewall's speech, the meeting passed several resolutions, including one asserting, "That clause of the U.S. Constitution which requires the surrender of a fugitive slave to his master, is not morally binding upon the American people, and should be disregarded."[11] In fact, Sewall proclaimed that there was "a higher law within us" that required aid to the runaway and the denial of the slaveholders' rights.[12] Well before New York antislavery Republican William Seward would publicly announce that a law higher than the Constitution guided northern opinion on the issue of slavery, Boston's abolitionists asserted that state laws opposing slavery trumped both the Fugitive Slave Clause and the 1793 Fugitive Slave Law.

The second issue of the *Latimer Journal*, a newspaper initiated to support Latimer's release, defended Massachusetts's borders and argued that its rights as a state were being violated by the fugitive slave crisis. James Freeman Clarke argued that the Latimer affair was awakening northerners to the fact "that the question of slavery is one which *does* belong to them," suggesting that abolitionists believed the Latimer case represented a fundamental turning point in northern opinion on slavery.[13] In an article optimistically titled "The Signs of the Times," the *Latimer Journal* claimed that the Latimer affair led northerners to reevaluate their connections to slavery. Just ten years prior to Latimer's arrest, only a handful of African American activists would be aroused by the rendition of a fugitive. But thanks to the furor over Latimer, "now . . . thousands . . . of the most intelligent and religious minds in Massachusetts" came out of their homes to object.[14] Echoing the optimism, Garrison argued in *The Liberator*, "'What has the North to do with slavery?' Dare any man now have the effrontery to ask this question."[15]

As African Americans and their abolitionist allies had hoped, a remarkable series of meetings erupted across the state to dispute Latimer's arrest and to defend the state's right to ignore the federal fugitive slave laws.[16] "Latimer meetings" took place throughout Massachusetts and even spread to other New England towns. One of the first and boldest of these town meetings, held at the Lyceum Hall in Lynn in early November 1842, gathered men and women, African Americans and whites, to denounce angrily Latimer's imprisonment. Lynn's protestors argued, "To come upon our territory and seize our citizens, without form or process of law, IS AN ACT OF WAR."[17] As Lynn made clear, the debate over Latimer's case was not an abstract introduction of a higher law ideology that would later become a hallmark of political abolitionism. Rather, the resolutions adopted in Lynn specifically pointed to rights being taken away by the national compromise over slavery.

As white and black activists already knew, and as ordinary free-state citizens were coming to believe, the Latimer case was never about one self-emancipated slave but instead symbolized the broader political, moral, and legal battle between the states. Papers across free-soil states took note of the developments and recognized the magnitude of the crisis.[18] Though of course no one knew at the time, the fighting and killing on a massive scale during the American Civil War was still almost twenty years in the future. Yet, as we saw in chapter 1, as early as the 1820s, free and slave states were already locked in fierce conflict over the nature of borders, a conflict that had intensified by the time of Latimer's seizure.

Both sides of the debate over George Latimer's fate saw the case extending far beyond private interests. "This is not an individual matter, which may be compromised or hushed up," the *Norfolk Herald* declared. "It is the case of every slaveowner in the South." In fact, the paper argued, Massachusetts violated "the compact between the States," which for "all intents and purposes [had been] DISSOLVED" by the state's actions. If the Constitution and federal laws could be "nullified by the laws of Massachusetts, or the insurrectionary proceedings of her citizens, with impunity," the newspaper claimed, then disunion necessarily followed.[19] Of course, "nullification" possessed powerful meaning in the South, since South Carolina had claimed the right to supersede federal laws inimical to its interests.[20]

The charge that northerners, and especially those in Massachusetts, had shifted their opinion on the constitutional obligation to return runaways was hard to deny, and in fact free-state commenters admitted that public opinion had changed. To underscore the swing in public opinion, citizens in Braintree, Massachusetts, avowed, "The compact of the Northern States with the Southern to deliver up the flying fugitive who seeks shelter and refuge among us . . . is a covenant with death."[21] Such an admission was obvious to keen contemporary observers. Just as the white South had become more absolute in its determination to defend bondage in the 1820s and especially after Nat Turner in the 1830s, northerners had also shifted in their stance on the legitimacy of the constitutional compromise over slavery. This evolution of public opinion was crucial for the sectional crisis, as northerners—like their southern compatriots—were coming to believe that the Union in its current form was no longer one to which they could declare moral or political allegiance. "The clause of the Constitution, providing for the surrender of fugitives from service," one Ohio editor wrote in the aftermath of the Latimer affair, "is daily becoming more and more repugnant to the feeling of the people of the free states." The editor admitted "freely and fully, that the [fugitive slave] provision of the Constitution" was no longer a compromise willingly upheld in many northern communities.[22] Massachusetts, and especially Boston, remained inflamed by the Latimer case for the next several years, passion that only intensified after the Fugitive Slave Law passed Congress as part of the Compromise of 1850.[23]

The "Final Settlement": The Compromise of 1850

The year 1850 opened with building fear that the national political crisis would soon lead to disunion. President Taylor was charged with leading the development of new states to come from the territories won under the Treaty of Guadalupe Hidalgo in 1848. Taylor's message sparked a reaction among southern members of the Congress. In February 1850 H. W. Hilliard of Alabama helped set the proslavery southern tone as it would evolve during the debate over the compromise bills. Hilliard asserted that the issue of whether slavery would be allowed in the new western lands was fundamentally a question of property rights. Since slaves were property, and since the Constitution placed no property above any other, southerners should have the right to bring slaves into the west. "It is no imaginary wrong of which we complain," Hilliard complained. "It is a colossal, overshadowing evil against which we contend."[24] Expressing a language and agenda that would dominate southern arguments over the western territories, Hilliard pointed out that the property rights of northerners should not be superior to the property rights of southerners.

By 1850, white southerners had long argued for greater protection of slavery and against abolitionism. The rise of abolitionists like Garrison in the 1830s and the controversies over slavery and the western territories during the war with Mexico had sharpened the southern defense of slavery into a well-worn tool. As the crisis escalated and as leading statesmen like Clay called for a new round of compromises that might ease the crisis, southerners stepped up their antiabolitionist and proslavery rhetoric. Such speeches often began with a historical recapitulation of all the issues that led to the present crisis, including the constitutional guarantees of protection for slavery that northerners, in the eyes of white southerners, trampled on.

Southern fire-eaters unleashed a torrent of racist, proslavery, and antiabolitionist rhetoric in the antebellum era. The language employed shocks the sensibilities of the modern reader, but it is important to realize that insults, epithets, and slurs were commonly heard in the halls of Congress. Years before the infamous caning of Charles Sumner in 1856, when the Massachusetts senator was beaten senseless over his verbal attack on southern slaveholders, the words used in the nation's capitol had reached unprecedented incivility. In his first speech before Congress, South Carolina representative John McQueen derided Massachusetts for criticizing slavery: "We reply to Massachusetts, that negroes are not citizens according to our law [and if] she may see fit to citizenize monkeys, it will furnish no reason why we should allow them such rights in the streets of Charleston."[25]

Many northerners and southerners thought the attempt at compromise futile and dangerous. Southern fire-eaters already clamored for secession even as Clay, Webster, Douglas, and others worked hard to forge a settlement. William Henry Trescot, a prominent diplomat and writer from South Carolina, advocated secession in 1850 as "the only safety of the South."[26] Trescot argued that through bondage the South had solved the common problem of all modern nations: the problem of labor versus capital. Chiding northerners for ignoring the underclass within their own midst, the masses of ill-housed, poorly paid, and overworked immigrant laborers, Trescot and other southern thinkers claimed that they had discovered a way around the labor strife that periodically consumed northern businesses and cities. Slaves were in no position to form unions, go on strike, or organize a workplace disturbance. In fact, Trescot and likeminded southerners asserted, free societies were proving to be miserable failures, and if they were smart they would adopt slavery and end labor problems once and for all.

What Trescot and his fellow southerners failed to realize was that abolitionists did not necessarily defend the North even as they attacked slavery. They knew well that northern industries treated their laborers miserably, and they knew that authorities put down strikes and other disturbances with crushing brutality. Many abolitionists wanted better treatment for northern workers as well as the end of southern slavery. Southerners were so busy defending slavery that they assumed northern abolitionists defended unflinchingly the conditions of immigrant laborers in Boston or New York. Yet abolitionists rarely defended such conditions and many strove for the betterment of the poor in both regions.

Regardless of their views on industrial capitalism, northern abolitionists and southern fire-eaters agreed that by 1850 disunion was a real and palpable possibility. While white southerners had been complaining of abolitionist criticism and what they perceived to be northern fanaticism since the early nineteenth century, threats of disunion were not mere rhetorical flourishes or hyperbole. After the U.S.-Mexican War and the announcement of the Wilmot Proviso, southern frustration with northern free-soil politicians had led many to declare that secession was imminent. Northern free-soil politicians dismissed such claims. Salmon P. Chase declared, "Least of all does the stale cry of disunion alarm me."[27] Congressmen had heard such cries for decades, and they might have dismissed such warnings as nothing more than hot-blooded demagogues trying to appeal to voters back home. But even many moderate southerners who thought disunion would be a disaster warned that their congressional colleagues were not just blowing smoke. In private letters to friends and relatives back home, southern politicians feared that unless northerners fully recognized the South's right to bring slaves into the western territories and settled satisfactorily the questions of the Texas boundary and California, then southern constituents would demand that their representatives force the Union to break up. Representative Albert Gallatin Brown of Mississippi warned northern leaders like Chase not to dismiss talk of disunion as empty rhetoric: "Gentlemen [of the North] tell us they do not believe the South is in earnest. They believe we will submit. Let me warn them to put away that delusion."[28]

It is difficult to gauge southern public opinion on these questions. No doubt white southerners adamantly believed that they should have the right to bring their slave property into the Southwest and California. There is also little doubt that white southerners, particularly those in the border states, were frustrated by the constant flow of runaway slaves who made their way to freedom. But whether or not such irritation meant that the majority of white southerners favored disunion in 1850 is a harder question to answer. By most accounts, whites in the Upper South were not prepared to advocate secession, while many more (perhaps even a majority) in the Deep South favored secession. In announcing his support for some sort of compromise to ease sectional tensions, South Carolina's William J. Grayson argued, "There is no unmistakable evidence of a conviction on the part of our people that they can no longer continue their social, civil and political relations with the Northern States."[29] Despite the rhetoric of radical abolitionists and fire-eating secessionists, southerners worried over the destruction that a civil war might bring. In a meeting in Bibb County, Georgia, in late September 1850, citizens supported the Compromise of 1850 and expressed concern that war would have "disastrous consequences," lead to "mischief and ruin," and "absorb all [their] resources."[30]

As Americans read in their town newspapers about the compromise debates, and specifically about Clay's proposals, they acted quickly to affect the outcome of the potential legislation. Nineteenth-century Americans were avid newspaper readers, and each city and town could boast of at least one newspaper and often two or more. Papers published on a daily, weekly, biweekly, or triweekly basis proliferated in rural areas as well as towns. Journalists were not taught to value objectivity as they are in modern journalism schools, and reporters often deliberately slanted the news to fit one side of the debate. Political parties established newspapers to promote specific candidates or campaigns, often with the party promoted dramatically in an elaborate masthead. Newspapers also promoted specific religious sects, reform efforts like temperance, or secretive groups like the Masons. Postal records from the era before the Civil War also show that Americans subscribed not just to their local newspapers but to periodicals from outside their region. Southerners subscribed avidly to Philadelphia, New York, and Boston papers, despite the fact that they might carry the taint of abolitionism. And northerners subscribed to national periodicals like Baltimore's *Niles Weekly Register* for inside stories on Washington politics.

Almost as soon as Clay laid out the key issues of the admission of California, the Texas boundary, the need for a new fugitive slave law, and the questions of slavery in the southwestern territories, Americans began writing newspaper editorials, giving speeches and sermons, and authoring pamphlets to influence debates. Impassioned voters were not about to let their congressmen debate the compromise proposals without persistent and direct input from back home. The *Journal of Commerce* and *The Independent*, two New York newspapers, engaged in a running editorial debating the merits of the compromise. The *Journal of Commerce* angrily denounced the right of the clergy to preach politics from the pulpit, and *The Independent* defended that right. Many moderate and conservative northerners had grown weary of ministers' involvement in political debate, and they spoke out against religious "fanaticism" that had found a home in abolitionism. In particular the two papers dueled on the question of the proposal for a new law to recapture runaway slaves. In an April 1850 editorial, *The Independent* declared that northerners would not obey the law if passed, claiming, "The people are opposed to slave catching on free soil. . . . Ten thousand pulpits are every week pouring light upon the public mind. . . . And Daniel Webster might as well pour oil on Niagara to calm it."[31] The *Journal of Commerce* reflected the views of many northern businessmen who wanted the compromise to pass. They viewed talk of disunion as bad for trade between North and South and knew that even a brief civil war harbored disastrous consequences for business. In response to *The Independent*, the *Journal of Commerce* asked, "If there are objections against clergymen's meddling with politics out of the pulpit, what shall be said of those who bring politics into the pulpit, on the Sabbath!"[32] State legislatures, too, got into the act. They drafted specific instructions to their senators and representatives on how they expected the congressmen to vote. On the same day that Webster delivered his famous address in support of the compromise, Indiana legislators instructed their congressmen to vote for a law "forever excluding" slavery from any territory acquired from the war with Mexico.[33] By May 1850 the outlines of a possible compromise were becoming clear, thanks in large part to the efforts of Stephen Douglas and a handful of others.[34]

During the summer, members had a chance to return home and discuss the compromise with their constituents. Virginia's John Minor Botts spoke at a dinner at Powhatan Courthouse attended by three hundred Whigs from around the state. Even moderates like Botts had to be clear: they opposed the Wilmot Proviso and would vote against it a thousand times if need be. But, Botts argued, just because he opposed the proviso did not mean he rejected the power of Congress over the territories.[35]

Relatively moderate southern politicians like Botts were still vexed on how to deal with the question of slavery in the West.

In part to provide southern congressmen with some direction, a meeting of delegates from throughout the region met in June in Nashville. Originally suggested by southern political leaders like Calhoun, the Nashville Convention met in the sweltering summer of 1850 to discuss what steps to take if the debates in Congress resulted in the prohibition of slavery in the western territories acquired from the U.S.-Mexican War. Congress had been debating the compromise resolutions since January, and leaked information about the substance of the debates often generated rumors about a new version of the Wilmot Proviso. In part to head off any congressional maneuvers or compromises to keep slavery out of the western lands and in part to have a plan in place should Congress move in that direction, seven slave states sent delegates to Nashville to discuss possible reactions.

At first, it appeared that the fire-eaters might prevail at the convention. After all, the meeting had been suggested by Calhoun, long known as a secessionist. Louisiana politicians had been so concerned that the delegates might side with disunion that they prevented their state's delegates from traveling to Nashville. The rhetoric at the meeting seemed to give validity to Louisiana moderates' concerns.

On June 8, the convention adopted a series of resolutions to lay out the views of the slave states on the compromise measures being debated in Congress. The key resolution stated, "The territories of the United States belong to the people of the several States of this Union as their common property," so free states had no right to prevent slavery from the territories.[36] For southerners, the most important point was that slaves were property, and slave owners enjoyed the ability to carry their chattel property, just like all other forms of property, from farm animals and implements to clothing and guns, into western lands. In fact, of the twenty-eight resolutions passed by the convention, the majority zeroed in on the property rights of slave owners, rights that should not be abridged or eliminated "in favor of the proprietors of other property against them."[37] By other proprietors, the delegates meant northern businessmen and farmers, who were allowed to take all of their property with them as they moved west. What really angered white southerners was the possibility that they would be treated unequally or as second-class citizens; in the slave owners' views, the government had no role to play in deciding which citizens to place above others. Under the existing laws, slaves were property, and ownership brought the right to be treated on a par with owners of all other types of property. Of course, the slave owners saw no irony or contradiction in making their case for equality under the law. Fairness and justice was theirs to be had, even as they deprived their slaves of those same rights to equality under the law. In the convention's published report to the South, we see the same emphasis on rejecting the Wilmot Proviso and on asserting the rights of southerners to take their slave property into the new western lands. The same cry that slave owners are being treated as second-class citizens pervades the address. "Where is that respect and comity," the delegates ask, that equal citizens are due in the nation?[38]

Although claims to equal treatment as property owners governed the sentiment of the Nashville Convention delegates, they made other concerns known as well. Along with the usual calls to oppose "Northern fanatics," calls that populated virtually all antebellum southern speeches, sermons, or editorials, the delegates also supported the prompt resolution of the Texas boundary question. Perhaps most stunning was the resolutions' claims that "slavery exist[ed] in the United States independent of the Constitution."[39] Although the resolutions do not refer directly to William Henry Seward's declaration that abolitionists followed a "higher law" than the Constitution, the Nashville delegates themselves came very close to saying the same thing. If slavery existed beyond the reach of the Constitution and human laws, as the Nashville delegates claimed, then slavery was subject to limitation and even abolition outside national laws, as Seward argued.

Only one resolution dealt with the issue of "the restoration of fugitives from service or labor," but the statement was brief and vague. The convention report added little to the discussions of the fugitive slave problem. The delegates understood as a result of the report published by the Committee of Thirteen in Congress that a new fugitive slave law might become part of the compromise package. But even the potential new law was not enough to satisfy the delegates. "There can be no concession or favor to the South," they argued, "in giving her only what she has a right to have under the Constitution."[40] The new more powerful fugitive slave law was intended to appease southerners in return for the abolition of the slave trade in Washington, D.C., and other parts of the compromise. But clearly the delegates did not feel appeased.

Although Virginia senator James Mason was at the same time demanding a new and stronger fugitive slave law, the Nashville delegates were more interested in their rights to carry slave property into western territories. While this might seem odd, a glance at the membership of the Nashville Convention provides a clue to the seeming contradiction. The loudest calls for a new law to return runaway slaves came from the southeastern states along the Atlantic Coast, especially Georgia and the Carolinas, and the Upper South states like Maryland and Virginia. Yet the delegates meeting in Tennessee came mostly from that state as well as from other more westerly states like Arkansas, Missouri, Texas, Alabama, and Mississippi. Their interests lay in the lands farther to their west.

Southerners along the Atlantic seaboard continued to bemoan the loss of slavery property, and James B. DeBow, one of the region's leading statisticians, published an estimate on how many slaves had run away. Using the calculations first offered by a Virginia commenter, DeBow argued that between 1810 and 1850, more than sixty thousand enslaved people had fled the South for freedom in the North, or more than fifteen hundred per year on average. DeBow argued that the free states owed the slave states an average per capita value of $450, almost $28 million in total.[41]

It is ironic, perhaps, that the congressional debates from January to September focused so much on California, Texas, and the Wilmot Proviso, and relatively so little time was spent discussing the Fugitive Slave Law. For almost as soon as the president signed the law and it became public, the debate shifted dramatically. Among the free states, the most powerful storm surrounded not the West or the Southwest but the new law to facilitate the recapture of runaway slaves.

Clay's speech before Congress in support of the compromise measures, though dramatic, did not achieve the desired result, and almost immediately his proposals for compromise came under withering scorn from both parties and both sections. Still, the speech did successfully establish an agenda for Congress to consider. The main issues Clay laid out—California statehood, the existence of slavery in the western territories that had been gained from the war with Mexico, the boundaries of Texas, the existence of slavery in the nation's capital, and the additional concern over fugitive slaves—framed the outline of the congressional debates for the next several months, from the end of January until September.

California, Texas, and Slavery in the West

The admission of California into the Union as a free state was a key sticking point. The gold rush had brought tens of thousands of settlers to the lands along the Pacific Coast, and San Francisco had grown dramatically in size and population. So many forty-niners moved to California that its citizens had the option of foregoing territorial status altogether and applying for statehood directly. Southerners wanted to delay the admission of California by forcing it to go through a transitional period as a territory before it became a state. They knew that few slaves worked in California, and a delay might give southerners the chance to bring in greater numbers of slaves and increase the likelihood that it would eventually enter the Union with slavery protected. White southerners thought they had an ally in President Taylor, who owned more than a hundred slaves in Mississippi and who lived in Louisiana at the time of his election as president in 1848. Southerners were deeply disappointed, therefore, when Taylor came out for the immediate admission of California into the Union as a free state. Taylor reasoned that, by admitting California quickly, he could avoid heated debates later on about the status of slavery there. If he moved ahead now, few could dispute the prediction that the new state's constitution would outlaw slavery.

White southerners were shocked and dismayed by Taylor's stance. They continued to press for greater protection for slavery, particularly the ability for slave owners to settle in the western territories. Pierre Soule of Louisiana refused to support the bills in late May because, in his view, the South gave up too much in admitting California as a free state and excluding slavery from much of the Southwest. "I will not seem to be contented," Soule declared before the Senate, "with terms which, under the *name* of compromise, take all and yield nothing. I cannot seem to approve, and still less can I give my public assent to that which I think is neither just, fair, or kind."[42]

Senator James M. Mason of Virginia called for the permanent extension of the 36°30' line (also known as the Missouri Compromise line) to the Pacific, with slavery permitted south of the line. In his May 27 speech, Mason agreed with Calhoun that the admission of California as a free state was inimical to southern interests, but he also gave his personal opinion, much to Clay's surprise, that he would support the western extension of the 36°30' line.[43] Unfortunately for Clay, Mason did not speak for the rest of the South, who, Clay feared, would not agree to such a settlement.

On February 8, Texas senator Sam Houston, already a legend for his military exploits in the West, rose, but after beginning his speech, he had to pause to accommodate the "many ladies waiting without . . . who were anxious to hear" his remarks.[44] As the ladies filed in, Houston began his speech before the Senate chamber. Houston immediately claimed that Congress had no power to prevent slavery in the territories, a claim that other southern politicians would take up again and again in the following months of debate. Instead, Houston argued in favor of popular sovereignty, that idea that would prove a failure in Kansas in the mid-1850s but which still appealed to the nation's democratic sympathies. Houston thought that the residents of the new states, in forming their first constitution, should be able to determine the status of slavery. Even this nod to democracy did not appeal to many southerners, however, who feared that property rights in slaves might be cancelled or overruled by democratic fiat. But as a moderate southerner, Houston saw popular sovereignty as the best means of deciding the question. Although the ladies had flocked to the chamber to hear Houston speak, popular sovereignty would not be the tactic employed by his fellow southerners, many of whom questioned democracy as the means to solve such a thorny and emotional issue as slavery.

Southerners saw an opportunity to press the proslavery case and please voters back home. John C. Calhoun, aging and with a long career now behind him, rose feebly before Congress on March 4. Abolitionist agitation, Calhoun argued, certainly irritated the white South and led them to consider disunion. But the real cause of secessionist sentiment in the region was due to the larger issue of federal power, "that the equilibrium between the two sections in the government . . . [had] been destroyed."[45] The imbalance in population, Calhoun asserted, provided northerners with more political power, which they in turn had used to subjugate the South and attack slavery. At the same time, the government had greatly expanded its powers, he maintained, and expanding population and power led to vile proposals like the Wilmot Proviso. And in Calhoun's opinion the compromise bills before Congress were nothing more than "a modification of the Wilmot Proviso."[46] He rejected outright the notion that California should enter the Union as a free state, and he vigorously defended the South's right to take slaves into the western territories. Any talk of a free California or the right of Congress to exclude slavery from the territories, Calhoun argued, was simply enshrining the ideas behind the proviso.

Few southern moderates could be trusted to help sway regional opinion. John Bell of Tennessee was a moderate who would go on to reject secession during the 1860 presidential election when he ran with the compromising Constitutional Union Party. In his speech before the Senate in early July, Bell traced the history of the controversy over slavery and the rise of sectional animosity. Like most southerners, Bell lay special blame at the feet of "the fanatics and sentimentalists of the North," the abolitionists who placed more importance on the supposed suffering of the slave than on the preservation of the Union.[47] Although modern observers often think of the South as the Bible Belt, as a bastion of strong religious devotion, many politicians in the 1850s blamed religious fervor for fueling abolitionism. Bell saw religion as the enemy of calm, rational thought, and like other southerners, he pointed out that many leading abolitionists were northern ministers. In this lot he also cast sentimentalists, especially women, who through some nervous system malfunction became obsessed with the suffering of others. These abolitionists harbored "a morbid sensibility" and were likely "recluses—readers and authors of sentimental literature, who cannot bear the contemplation of the inevitable ills and hardships of real life."[48] These were common insults hurled at abolitionists, especially antislavery women, by northerners and southerners. But in his speech during the debate over the Compromise of 1850, Bell made clear that he was no fire-eater. He intended to "hold fast to the Constitution," and he hoped "that some final adjustment of all these distracting questions will yet be devised and adopted."[49] Bell supported slavery and thought that slave owners should be allowed to settle in the western territories. But he also came down in favor of a compromise that would preserve the Union.

The moderates tried mightily to sway their colleagues' opinions, but southerners like Mississippi senator Jefferson Davis remained opposed to the compromise measures. Davis and his fellow Mississippi senator Henry Foote engaged in a heated debate on the Senate floor near the end of June that indicated just how difficult a compromise would be. Foote and Davis exchanged charges and countercharges of promoting secession, alternately interrupting one another for more than two hours. Davis was steadfastly opposed to the compromise, particularly to any stipulation that prevented slavery in the West, and he defended his right to reject the compromise. Foote, in common with other Unionist southerners, claimed that the fire-eaters were as fanatical as the abolitionists. This claim Davis did not deny: "It is charged here and elsewhere that the ultras [extremists] of the North and the South have met, and that this great and important measure of settlement and compromise is to be destroyed by that conjunction."[50] If that was true, Davis declared, then so be it.

Northern Democrats like Michigan's Lewis Cass denounced the southern rhetoric angrily and pushed for compromise. Cass resented the calls for disunion by fire-eating senators like Davis, and he knew that if the "ultras" had their way, then no compromise would come. Cass avoided taking on Calhoun on all of the points in the South Carolinian's speech, but one statement Cass could not avoid. In his speech Calhoun had referred to George Washington as an "illustrious southerner." Cass wrangled with this statement, claiming that Calhoun did not refer to "the renowned warrior—not the eminent statesman—not the distinguished citizen—not the great American—not the beloved Virginian—but the illustrious southerner!"[51] Northerners and southerners by 1850 could not even agree on how to remember the father of the country.

Free-soil members of Congress shared their unhappiness with the compromise with a vehemence matching the ire of southern fire-eaters. One of the Senate's fiercest critics of slavery was Ohioan Salmon P. Chase, who had already earned a reputation for defending runaway slaves in danger of recapture and for his firm stance in abolitionist ranks. Near the end of March, Chase rose to give his speech on Clay's compromise proposals. Chase did not claim that Congress had the power to abolish slavery in the South, but he did assert its authority "to prohibit its extension into national territories."[52] Chase argued that the Northwest Ordinance, passed in 1787 to govern the territories of Ohio and the surrounding region, was proof that Congress did have the authority to provide laws for new lands before they entered the Union as states. For Chase, Congress's power extended fully over the Southwest, and he denied southern claims that the Constitution supported slavery's extension into the West. When Senator Dawson rose to challenge Chase's claims, Chase responded that southerners had no right to interpret the Constitution. "Sir, when gentlemen from the slave states ask us to support the Constitution, I fear they mean only their *construction* of the Constitution."⁵³

But the most controversial speech given by the free-soil faction was William Henry Seward's March 11 speech against slavery. The New York Whig senator already had a well-earned reputation for abolitionism, having served as governor of the nation's most populous state. His political visibility made him widely known and despised in the South. But Seward's "Higher Law" speech, as it became known, was harshly condemned by northern as well as southern Democrats. Michigan Democrat Lewis Cass announced on the Senate floor that it was "one of the most disingenuous I have ever heard."⁵⁴ In reply, Seward remarked that "the natural ally of slavery in the South, was the Democracy [Democratic Party] of the North."⁵⁵ The stinging rebuke of northern Democrats like Cass for being the lackeys of southern slaveholders created further accusations on the floor. Yet there was some strong element of truth in Seward's claim, as northern "doughface" politicians were well-known for making common cause with the South to promote the Democratic Party and its interests.

As the Democrats well knew, the longer the debate over the compromise bills continued, the more divided between its northern and southern wings the party became. Democrat Thomas Hart Benton tried to table the whole set of compromises devised by the Committee of Thirteen in mid-June, hoping to stave off further divisions until March of the following year. "It is time to be done with this comedy of errors," said Benton, characterizing the debates over the compromise, "[and postpone] this unmanageable mass of incongruous bills" to the next congressional session.⁵⁶ Benton's recommendation was not followed, and the debate continued. The Senate leadership, including Clay, Webster, and Douglas, felt that they had gone too far—had laid their careers and reputations on the line—to turn back now or postpone the controversies.

The Fugitive Slave Law

While southerners like Bell were incensed over a free California and the possible exclusion of slavery from the western territories, others stepped up their criticism of the North for failing to return runaway slaves. Southerners claimed with some justification that the Fugitive Slave Clause of the Constitution had been rejected in spirit and in practice by northern politicians. The personal liberty laws were devised as an explicit rejection of the clause and of the 1793 Fugitive Slave Act after the Supreme Court's decision in *Prigg v. Pennsylvania*. Northern communities made clear that they would not cooperate in fulfilling the requirements of the Constitution's clause or the 1793 law. In return, southerners asserted that they wanted to uphold the Union and the Constitution while abolitionists worked to undermine them. One Virginian remarked, "So far from executing this clause, and 'delivering up' the runaway slaves, the free states refuse to pass any efficient law to that end in Congress." In fact, argued this Virginian, "Their whites and free negroes assemble in mobs to rescue the slave from the master who is bold enough to capture him."[57] Southerners faced mortal danger in attempting to recapture their property, leading Thomas Clingman of North Carolina to estimate that the region had lost $15 million worth of slaves to the North since 1787. In the eyes of many southerners, especially those in the Upper South states of Virginia and Maryland, where proximity to the North made running away easier, the fugitive slave problem was just as acute as the question of slavery in the Mexican cession.

Free-soil politicians like Chase and Seward denounced the Fugitive Slave Act, but northern Democrats favoring compromise knew that no settlement would be possible without it. Michigan senator Cass wanted to use the fugitive slave measure to assuage the South, as a "pledge of [the North's] sincerity, and of [its] desire to do justice to that great section of [the] common country."⁵⁸ In his "Higher Law" speech, New York Senator Seward had harshly criticized the proposal for a new fugitive slave law as unworkable and antithetical to the wishes of northern voters. Seward had argued that the Fugitive Slave Clause of the Constitution was immoral, an argument that infuriated Cass, who declared, "No man should come here, who believes that ours is an immoral Constitution; no man should come here, and, by the solemn sanction of an oath, promise to support an immoral Constitution."

That the Fugitive Slave Law would be the most hotly contested provision of the Compromise of 1850 surprised nearly everyone, including Clay, Webster, and Douglas. They simply could not understand why so many northern "fanatics" (as they called them) thought that a law so clearly just—one that in fact reaffirmed a clause of the Constitution—could evoke such powerful passions. But thousands of northerners were in fact infuriated by the law, including many erstwhile moderates who had considered slavery to be merely a "southern problem." An acerbic Ralph Waldo Emerson, once a Webster admirer, declared that "the word *liberty* in the mouth of Mr. Webster sounds like the word *love* in the mouth of the courtesan."⁵⁹ Yet, while scholars have often pointed to northerners' fury over the law and Webster's supposed betrayal for supporting the compromise, they have not recognized the extent to which dissatisfaction with the compromise contributed significantly to a growing distrust of politicians and even suspicion of the very idea of compromising with the South to save the Union. Emerson, who had remained largely aloof from abolitionism in the 1830s and 1840s, experienced a change after 1850, pointing to the Fugitive Slave Law as the cause of his conversion to abolitionism.⁶⁰

Emerson was not alone in his disgust with Webster. Historians of the Second Party System have often pointed to a powerful strain of "antipartyism" running through national ideology in the late antebellum era. In his classic *The Political Crisis of the 1850s*, Michael Holt argued that ideological convergence between Whigs and Democrats on economic matters like government activism, especially in funding internal improvements like railroads and banks, weakened party allegiance.[61] But a powerful strain of antiparty sentiment can be traced directly to the compromise and the Fugitive Slave Law. Abolitionist and pro-Union northerners alike charged that the fury over the law proved the impossibility of compromise to save the Union, the inherent corruption of the party system, and the demagogic nature of political leaders. The country had been taken over, one pro-Union northerner complained, "by *demagogues who want votes*, and *politicians* who want *place* and *power*. . . . Both parties [had] been poisoned and corrupted and their conservative principles abandoned by the leaders of *sections* of each."[62] In Worcester in October 1850, just weeks after the Fugitive Slave Law became public, Charles Allen remarked, to shouts of "Shame! Shame!" from his audience, that everywhere he saw "expressions of anxiety and of determination upon the countenances of men. . . . Every free state in this Union [was] deeply excited [and] indignant at the existing state of things." Politicians, Allen charged, passed the Fugitive Slave Law only after "calculat[ing] the chances of the election of this man or that man."[63] New York's antislavery *Independent* newspaper declared that "compromises dictated by wily politicians, made to serve in a pinch in party tactics . . . to whom spoils are virtues and offices religion" were not to be followed.[64]

In a typical northern abolitionist response to the passage of the law, the Reverend Arthur Dearing declared, "Great legislators resolve by 'compromise' that injustice shall be *justice*[, and] herds of hungry politicians . . . gather around our capital with both hands in the public treasury . . . [and] flatter or frown a majority into their favorite schemes." In such a time, Dearing asserted, the voters were duty-bound to take down the politicians and their parties. "Resistance to the slaveholder," Dearing argued, "is the same in kind which Washington made against British aggression and servitude."[65] Writing from New York City, Benjamin Seaver complained in the wake of the arrest of one suspected runaway, "[There is] so little principle in these compromising politicians, that I shall not be surprised at anything. When a nation undertakes to *compromise* a wrong it always begets [ill consequences] either in the present, or [in] successive generations."[66] In the midst of debate about what would become the Fugitive Slave Law, African American abolitionist Samuel Ringgold Ward, referring to compromise, agreed, "There is no term which I detest more than this, it is always the term which makes right yield to wrong; it has always been accursed since Eve made the first *compromise* with the devil."[67] It is not surprising that opposition to compromise emanated from immediate abolitionists, but the distrust of parties, politicians, and the notion of compromise spread far beyond radical abolitionism and penetrated into the heart of American culture.

Yet, as we will see, the Fugitive Slave Law also had powerful and vocal defenders in the free states, not the least of whom included leaders of both of the national political parties. Even as many free-state residents protested the statute, Douglas, Webster, and other prominent pols called for the North and Midwest to abide by the compromise. In late 1850 and early 1851, free soil became a hotly contested territory between the procompromise and anticompromise forces, bitterly dividing northern communities and creating civil conflict over whether to adhere to the Union and the constitutional compromise over slavery.

CHAPTER THREE

Civil Conflict in the North

Reactions to the Fugitive Slave Law in the Fall of 1850

In March 1850, while the nation's capital buzzed with debates over a series of bills that would emerge as the Compromise of 1850, Peyton Polly's haunting nightmares became reality in a small midwestern village far from Washington, D.C. An African American man who resided with his seven children and one grandchild in southern Ohio, Polly lived in constant fear of being kidnapped. On March 6, the day before Massachusetts senator Daniel Webster would deliver his famous speech in favor of the Fugitive Slave Act, a gang of white kidnappers axed their way into Polly's home, beat him severely, and dragged his eight young charges across the border into Kentucky.[1] Quickly and with bloodless efficiency, the gang sold four of the children to slave traders in Kentucky and whisked the other four to Virginia. Ohio governor Salmon P. Chase sent agents to recover the children and, after three agonizing years, finally secured the return of those held in Kentucky, but the others toiled in slavery until the end of the Civil War.

The Polly family story is but one of thousands of similarly horrific instances of racial violence in antebellum America. As chapter 2 began to show, the Fugitive Slave Law threw northern communities into furious activity, and new historical work on the rescue of runaway slaves reminds us that African Americans vigorously resisted enforcement of the law throughout the Northeast and Midwest. Boston, Philadelphia, Milwaukee, New York, Detroit, Syracuse, Worcester, and other towns erupted in violence as white federal and local officials sought to enforce the Fugitive Slave Law against a loose coalition of abolitionists and ordinary African Americans determined to defy it.[2] The Polly case, along with hundreds of similar instances of abduction, brought the struggle over free and slave borders to the forefront of the sectional crisis, sparking a legal conflict that reflected similar interstate clashes across the country. The small struggle of this family became, in the words of one historian, "a battle between Ohio and Virginia."[3]

The passage of the Fugitive Slave Law as part of the Compromise of 1850 not only created political conflict between the free and slave states but also deeply divided northerners and midwesterners themselves, sparking a series of rallies and counterrallies and a furious discussion over the nature of republican government not seen since the original debates over the Constitution. Massachusetts reverend L. H. Sheldon declared, "It is to this law that all thoughts are now turned. The great question with all good men is, what shall *I* do in regard to it?"[4] The tremendous uproar over the Fugitive Slave Law enveloped the free states as soon as it became public.

Northern states and their towns were riven by schisms over the law, as old friends became estranged and communities divided over their responsibilities to abide by the law. The debate within the free states over the Fugitive Slave Law led northerners to rethink their relationship with the federal government. Sermons, political speeches, newspaper editorials, and family discussions all turned on key questions: What duty did citizens have to uphold laws they deemed unjust? Which was more important, maintaining the constitutional compromise with the South over returning runaways, or protecting the rights of northern states to keep slavery out of their borders? Was the

Constitution itself worth saving, or did it require one to compromise one's principles too much? Between late September 1850 and the first months of 1851, free-state citizens and their political leaders considered what the new law meant for the future of the republic.

Thanks to the work of black petitioners who insisted that their fundamental rights as free citizens be secured, white political leaders had to confront an embarrassing truth: "free soil" would have little meaning if state lines could be crossed with impunity by slave catchers. Massachusetts pastor William C. Whitcomb decried the law before his congregation: "Fellow-citizens and Christian friends, the new Fugitive Law . . . will *enslave you and me* as well as the *black* man—It will make slaves of us all. Talk not of the *Free States*! There are none such now!"[5] The unprecedented rage in 1850–51 among many northerners and westerners—especially those who had been undecided regarding the justice or injustice of slavery—raised the fortunes of abolitionists and permanently altered the political debate. The relatively new telegraph system meant that news spread almost instantaneously, and abolitionists knew that the new rapid form of communication could help swell their ranks.

Beginning in September 1850, when the Fugitive Slave Law first became public, telegraph wires burned with news of massive rallies and meetings to protest the despised legislation.[6] Thousands gathered in New York parks, Boston's Faneuil Hall, and Philadelphia's concert halls to hear rousing speeches about how the law had turned the North into one vast hunting ground for kidnappers. And as historian Tiya Miles demonstrates in her valuable new study, the controversy stretched far beyond the Northeast to cities like Detroit.[7] Abolitionists like George Thompson rejoiced. At a March 1851 antislavery convention in Syracuse, Thompson marveled at the turning tide. "Once, we were pelted with rotten eggs by an ignorant mob," he reminded his audience. "Now, we are pelted with . . . speeches from the Senate, House, and Presidential Proclamations. Once, we were laughed at by the lowly, scorned by the mighty, despised and derided by all. Now we are fast gaining the respect of the people. . . . Once, if the world heard anything of the Anti-slavery movement here they believed it was confined to half-a-dozen hot-headed fanatics and a few silly women. Now Europe rings with execrations against America for her Fugitive Slave Law."[8]

As Thompson's words suggest, outrage over the Fugitive Slave Law generated wide-ranging discussions about the meaning of freedom and citizenship. Everywhere northerners reacted with fury and scorn over the new legislation. In Trumbull County, angry Ohio voters passed more than a dozen resolutions denouncing the "greatly aggravated aggression of the slave power on our rights as citizens of a free state," resolving, "We will not, under any circumstances, render obedience [to it]."[9] Particularly galling, as the Trumbull County citizens pointed out, was the absence of any guarantees of trial by jury or habeas corpus protections, objections that were echoed in similar meetings of outraged midwesterners. At a similar meeting in Grant County, Indiana citizens decried the fact that the law "abridges the benefits of the writ of *habeas corpus* and *absolutely* refuses the right of trial by jury."[10] For free-state voters, the debate over the Fugitive Slave Law was not merely an abstraction; the law abrogated basic and long-standing rights that had long protected people from government power.

Not to be outdone by the newer states in the West and Midwest, northeasterners denounced the new runaway law in pulpits, in letters to newspapers, and in public speeches. In Connecticut, residents opposed to the Fugitive Slave Law declared the legislation an "unparalleled atrocity" and "a crime against humanity."[11] Citizens in Carbondale, Pennsylvania, announced publicly, "[Since the] Fugitive Slave Law is in direct violation of the commands of God, we are bound by a higher law."[12] Longtime observers could not compare the disruptions across the North and Midwest to any other experiences. Adams Jewett of Ohio stated clearly, "I have never seen such intense excitement pervade this community as now exists against the Fugitive Slave Law."[13] As Jewett and others in the free states knew well, not all were opposed to the new law. On the contrary, pro-Union voters believed strongly that defending and enforcing the law was essential to ensuring that the republic would endure. One Tennessee politician, in a letter to Pennsylvania Democrat James Buchanan, warned, "If the fugitive slave bill is not enforced in the North, there is no guessing what may be the consequences."[14] Buchanan and his fellow Democrats throughout the free states heeded the warning.

Enforcing the Law and Saving the Union

While fierce opposition to the Fugitive Slave Law emerged in late 1850, an opposition that generated a rethinking of the value of the Union itself among many northerners, an equally powerful movement to defend the compromise blossomed across the free states. Led primarily by Democrats and conservative Whigs, proponents of the law rallied to what they hoped would be a final end to the national schism over slavery. In fact, Clay, Webster, and other national political leaders billed the Fugitive Slave Act and the Compromise of 1850 as the absolute last word on the vexing problems facing the Union. While Emerson and other Massachusetts observers chastised Webster for supporting the settlement measures, others in New England praised the senator. A letter signed by dozens of citizens from Salisbury, New Hampshire, provided a boost to Webster and his fellow Unionists. "We are devoted to the Union as it is," the residents wrote Webster. "We adhere to the whole Constitution." Remembering that Webster "crushed nullification" during the debate with South Carolina two decades prior, these New Englanders expressed hope that it would be "Faction, and not the Union," that would be overthrown. Webster responded gratefully, remarking that he appreciated the support given, and saying, "In a critical hour, and not without some personal hazard, I have discharged my duty and freed my conscience."[15] Since he was being pilloried by northerners like Emerson for backing the compromise, Webster greatly valued the letter of encouragement.

Webster and other adherents to the compromise were not exaggerating when they admitted the "personal hazards" they bore in the months after the Fugitive Slave Law was announced, and they sought to ensure that the settlement would indeed be final. To counteract the overwhelmingly negative response to the legislation, Unionists rallied their voters to back the compromise. Rallies across the North in favor of the Union and specifically in favor of the Fugitive Slave Law supported the efforts to preserve the Union. One of the first such rallies, a so-called Great Union Demonstration, tried to counteract the anti–Fugitive Slave Law meetings of the fall. At the end of October 1850, some five thousand New Yorkers gathered at Castle Garden to promote the compromise measures. To present a bipartisan approach, three Whigs and three Democrats spoke at the meeting, "and all declared it the duty of the North and the whole country, to obey [the Fugitive Slave Law] in good faith."[16] White northerners delivered the speeches that evening, but white southerners would have found much to applaud. George Wood defended slavery strongly by stressing its supposedly civilizing influence over Africans. Slavery, thought Wood, would eventually die out in the southern states, but it would "need time to do so" and he was willing to wait.[17]

The New York Union rally made special appeals to the support of businessmen. The city was well known for its commercial ties to the cotton South as well as its lingering support for slavery. Although New York could count dedicated and passionate abolitionists among its citizens, it also was also a haven for Unionist and even proslavery and pro-South sympathies. James W. Gerard, an honored speaker at the New York rally, promised, "Merchants, traders, and mechanics of the empire city, your voice and actions of this night will be heard and felt throughout the length and breadth of this great Republic."[18] However, New York businessmen were sensitive to abolitionist claims that they thought commerce was more important than the sufferings of bondspeople. "It is said," remarked Charles O'Conor, "that the merchants of New York, have a pecuniary interest in southern trade, and are moved by sordid considerations. I repel and fling back the unjust reproach."[19] Yet, O'Conor made no apologies for the fact that the rally was specifically directed at New York businessmen, or for the fact that many of those in attendance came to protect their own financial interest in trading with the South.

Similar Unionist rallies soon erupted in small towns and large cities throughout the Midwest and Northeast, clashing with anticompromise supporters. Less than a month after New Yorkers assembled, a large procompromise meeting shook the early evening rafters at the Chinese Museum in Philadelphia. With a full band and with the museum decorated with banners proclaiming, "The Union Must and Shall Be Preserved!" and "Our Glorious Union," the event attracted supporters from around the region, including many businessmen. Nearly five thousand signed the official proceedings of the so-called Great Union Meeting, which fully backed the compromise measures, including the Fugitive Slave Act. Lewis Cass, James Buchanan, James Cooper, and Daniel Webster sent congratulatory and approving letters to the organizers of the rally. Future president James Buchanan argued from his home at Wheatland near Lancaster, Pennsylvania, "The honor of the South has been saved by the Compromise." He continued, "All that is necessary for us to do is to execute the Fugitive Slave Law, and to let the Southern people alone."[20]

Long-time politician George M. Dallas had the honor of addressing the Great Union Meeting in Philadelphia. Dallas believed, as did many others, that democracy itself was under attack in the controversy over slavery. He worried that secession and civil war would prove democracy's detractors correct: "No frame of government, fellow-citizens, is more difficult to construct than a Federal Union of Sovereign Republican States." Philosophers had long "regarded it in despair, as a social and political work, too arduous, if not impossible of attainment."[21] Dallas loudly proclaimed that the American republic, though it required compromise among local interests, had proven remarkably successful in encouraging prosperity and population growth. Like other supporters of the compromise, Dallas did not claim to approve of every measure passed or every pro-compromise speech given in Congress, but he did argue that keeping the states together required free-state and slave-state Americans to find middle ground. Referring specifically to the Fugitive Slave Law, Dallas affirmed in his dithyramb that the law was "in *perfect harmony with the Constitution of our country* . . . just to the fugitive, just to the claimant of his service, and just to the public."[22] As he read the Union meeting's resolutions aloud, Dallas received some of the loudest applause for those approving the Fugitive Slave Law. The Union meeting in Philadelphia, however, drew widespread scorn from abolitionists. The *Pennsylvania Freeman* called the meeting a "Great Demonstration of Northern Servility" that drew supporters "by appeals to avarice, political ambition, cowardly fears and selfish hopes." Though the paper noted that there were many attendees, the Union meeting did not embody the views of the voting public but instead represented "the selfish interests of business men and aspirants of political favor."[23]

Not be outdone, Boston Unionists held a mass meeting less than a week after Philadelphians celebrated their ties with the South. Once again, northern businessmen led the way. Announcements of the rally were posted in the Merchants' Reading Room to attract thousands of attendees. As had the Fugitive Slave Law's opponents, the supporters of the compromise gathered at Faneuil Hall in late November. Speaker John C. Warren, a veteran of the Revolution and of Bunker Hill, reminded his audience of "the prosperity which [they had] so long and happily enjoyed" in the Union.[24] Others like Thomas B. Curtis highlighted the fact that the Constitution was carefully crafted to protect slave property and that northerners had a duty to return runaways whether they agreed with rendition or not. Hour after hour, speakers rose to the podium to rally support for the Union, cognizant of the hall's place in the Revolutionary era.

The Boston rally at Faneuil Hall backing the settlement measures was echoed across the free states in late November. Thanksgiving was celebrated on different days in different parts of the country in 1850, for the national agreed-upon day in November had not yet been established. But regardless of which day the festivities were held that year, many speakers addressed the Compromise of 1850. Philadelphians held their Thanksgiving on December 12 and on that day invited Henry A. Boardman to deliver a pro-Union speech. Like other moderates, Boardman believed that the Union was not in peril for legitimate reasons, but rather because of the agitation caused by "a party at the South and another party at the North . . . inflamed with a bitter mutual hostility [who] have virtually joined hands for the purpose of demolishing this government."[25] Of particular concern to Boardman was the rancor over the Fugitive Slave Law, which he claimed was merely a reaffirmation of the Constitution's clause respecting runaways.

Northern supporters of the Fugitive Slave Law tried to refute objections that the new measure violated individual state authority or that it denied habeas corpus to suspected runaways. James A. Dorr, a New York lawyer, maintained that such fears were unfounded. In fact, Dorr avowed, the Fugitive Slave Law actually facilitated the suspected runaway's right to due process and habeas corpus. Section 6 of the law required a speedy meeting to judge the southerner's claim to ownership. "The substantial benefit of *habeas corpus*," he argued, "is the right to a speedy examination by a competent magistrate, of the legality or illegality of the imprisonment complained of."[26] Here Dorr was more than a bit disingenuous, for he knew that that part of the law was meant to aid the owner in a quick reclamation of his property, not to protect the rights of slaves. Dorr further maintained that denying slaves a right to trial by jury had always been sound policy. In any event, since slaves were not citizens by custom, they were not entitled to such protection. Moderate and conservative northerners like Dorr did not see anything in the Fugitive Slave Law that was new or alarming; he urged fellow northerners to see the law as merely an affirmation and strengthening of long-standing policies regarding runaways.

The deep rift within the white community in the free states threatened to erupt into civil conflict as cities in Ohio, Indiana, Massachusetts, and Pennsylvania experienced race riots and political upheaval.[27] Badly divided by internal conflict, the Common Council of Chicago denounced the Fugitive Slave Law in a series of resolutions, but when Stephen Douglas appeared before the council to defend the law, city leaders quickly reversed their vote.[28] City officials in Worcester, Massachusetts, were similarly divided over whether the new law gave a carte blanche to white criminality; the sheriff, the mayor, and local police differed vehemently on whether to enforce the right of whites to claim African Americans.[29] Pennsylvania's capital city was similarly riven with conflict over whether to support the new law. Initially the 1850 measure was treated with indifference or support, and throughout the decade, Harrisburg Democrats continued to support the Fugitive Slave Law as the lynchpin of the grand compromise. Other white Harrisburg citizens reacted angrily when the town's police force aided the federal marshals in returning runaways, and in 1854 city elections they voted out three of the town's four constables.[30] Support for or opposition to claims on African American freedom sharply cleaved the nation long before actual armies mobilized for the battlefield.

African Americans Fight Back against the Fugitive Slave Law

While free-state white voters clashed over the compromise measures, African American intellectuals and activists marshaled their forces to denounce the law. Black men and women, for example, gathered excitedly at the county courthouse in Philadelphia in late October to denounce the law. Speeches by local leaders of color like the Reverend H. D. Moore made clear that northern blacks would resist the law with violence if necessary.[31] These were not idle threats. When federal officials tried to arrest a black man in Detroit to demonstrate their intentions to enforce the law, hundreds of black residents armed themselves and tried to rescue the prisoner. Fearful of such a mob, authorities sent three companies of soldiers to Detroit to ensure the arrest would not be thwarted. Even so, angry black protesters threw brick-bats at the federal marshal and his carriage as they took the accused runaway to jail.[32] Similar riots erupted across the North and Midwest in cities like Springfield, Illinois, as the federal determination to enforce the law was met with equally vehement protests by both blacks and whites to obstruct the law's implementation.[33]

Mass meetings of black northerners erupted in response to the passage of the Fugitive Slave Law. "Nearly all the waiters in the hotels have fled to Canada," declared one Pittsburgh observer. On their way out of town, blacks "went in large bodies, armed with pistols and bowie knives, determined to die, rather than be captured."[34] In Columbus in early 1851, Ohio's people of color met to decide what action to take. Almost immediately a discussion ensued about whether the Constitution itself was hopelessly corrupted by its defense of bondage or whether the document and its commitment to democratic government could be employed to attack slavery. Cleveland's H. Ford Douglas considered the Constitution beyond repair, while William Howard Day argued that the problem lay with the interpretation of the Constitution.[35] In the wake of the Fugitive Slave Law, the debate between Douglas and Day was repeated across the free states. African Americans were unanimous, of course, in their denunciations of the act, but they were torn about how best to respond. Should they adhere only to the Declaration of Independence and its claim that "all men are created equal," or should they also embrace the Constitution through the political process?

As people of color in the free states wrestled with such intellectual considerations, they were simultaneously forced to deal with the kidnapping and renditions in real time in real communities. Although most northern blacks were barely literate, they devised elaborate warning systems to spread notice of kidnappers or slave hunters. William C. Nell, a leading black abolitionist in Rochester, New York, helped to convene a meeting of a city vigilance committee in 1851. The Rochester Anti-Fugitive Slave Law Committee, composed of leading black residents of the town, pledged to be "as watchful as Argus with his hundred eyes" and to "respond with the signal word [to] all within hearing" when someone was seized.[36] Once agreed upon, the signals could be put into practice when needed.

When Maryland slave owner Edward Gorsuch and his posse ventured into Christiana, Pennsylvania, to recapture William Parker, African Americans trumpeted a horn from a high window to sound the alarm. As Parker recalled, "It was a custom with us, when a horn was blown at an unusual hour, to proceed to the spot promptly to see what was the matter."[37]

Warning fellow African Americans of kidnappers and slave catchers in their midst helped potential victims prepare for battle or escape to a safer location, but once captured, an African American still held weapons with which to fight abduction. As we have seen, one of the most effective tactics was mobbing, in which African Americans would gather in sufficient numbers to overwhelm authorities and seize someone who had been taken to jail.[38] After the key Supreme Court case *Prigg v. Pennsylvania* (1842), personal liberty laws in many northern communities supposedly prevented state and local jailers from using public facilities to imprison the recaptured or the kidnapped, but such laws were often ignored or thwarted.[39] When a Kentucky slaveholder arrived in Detroit to claim a slave and his wife, a group of African Americans gathered at the jail where the accused runaways were held, overtook the jailers after a shootout with the sheriff, and ferreted the disguised couple away. For nearly a month the city remained under the control of federal troops sent by Secretary of War Lewis Cass.[40]

Similar incidents of mobbing erupted spontaneously across the country. The rescue of Shadrach Minkins in February 1851 came at the hands of Bostonians who noticed that constables had arrested Minkins after tricking him into believing that they were arresting him for petty thievery. The frightened Minkins quickly realized the real reason behind his detainment, but he was taken into custody. With the help of local Boston authorities, the accused runaway, terrified by the prospect of being returned to bondage, stood before a judge. But before a decision could be rendered, "a mob of Negroes broke into the courtroom and carried him off."⁴¹ When African Americans made a similar attempt to rescue Thomas Sims later in 1851 using the same mobbing technique that worked in the Minkins case, Boston officials and federal authorities were ready. President Millard Fillmore and Secretary of State Daniel Webster were determined to avoid a recurrence of the embarrassing ease with which a ragtag mob of African Americans had freed Minkins. With an overwhelming show of force, including a ring of armed troops surrounding the Boston courthouse, the mob was thwarted, Sims was returned to bondage, and the Fugitive Slave Law was upheld.⁴²

Outraged northern Unionists charged the "black mob" in the Minkins affair with treason. Conservative New England papers like the *New-Hampshire Patriot* argued that Boston's black community had been abetted by "white miscreants who profess to be governed by the 'high-law' of conscience." What irritated the conservative press even more was that "the whole freesoil press of the country are openly justifying and glorying over this infamous assault and triumph of a negro mob over the laws and constituted authorities of the land!"⁴³ Northern supporters of the compromise scorned the actions of black and white protestors because all knew that if the Fugitive Slave Law was to represent a "final settlement" of the long-standing slavery controversy, the law had to be upheld at all costs.

Acknowledging the importance of enforcing the Fugitive Slave Law, Henry Clay stood before the Senate in the wake of the Minkins rescue in early 1851 and strongly denounced the men who brought "odium on our laws and violate[d] justice and its officers." Clay's rebuke of the black and white activists who stormed the Boston courthouse was followed by a lengthy debate on the Senate floor over two days, with free-soil and Unionist senators sparring over whether or not the Fugitive Slave Law could or should be enforced. Interestingly, much of the criticism fell not on people of color who resisted the law but on white politicians and clergymen who had supposedly egged them on. Even Clay remarked, "These negroes are made the catspaw of miserable and designing men." Stephen Douglas then joined in, saying in reply to remarks by Salmon Chase that free-soil politicians in and out of the Senate "had produced in the minds of free negroes the impression that it was right and proper to resist the laws of the United States, when a *higher* law condemned the law of Congress."[44] What Clay and Douglas could not fully appreciate was the fact that people of color did not need white political leaders to lead the way in resisting unjust laws. Already by the 1850s, black activists across the North and Midwest had concluded that mob action was one legitimate way to combat a legal and political system that was so powerfully arrayed against them. While senators railed against the breaking of laws, African Americans knew that the law was unjust to begin with.

Despite admonitions on the Senate floor by eminent statesmen like Clay and Douglas, African Americans across the free states gathered each time a suspected runaway was captured or a black family stood in danger of kidnapping. Perhaps the most famous case of successful mobbing of northern African Americans, the "Jerry Rescue," erupted in Syracuse in October 1851 in the midst of the antislavery Liberty Party's convention being held in the city. Sympathizers, including black abolitionist J. W. Loguen, hid William Henry, a black artisan from Missouri known as Jerry, in Syracuse until Henry could escape into the Underground Railroad. Similar incidents erupted throughout the 1850s. In a riot in Worcester in 1854, a mixed-race mob found out that Asa O. Butman, a notorious Boston-based kidnapper, was staying in town. Surrounding the hotel, the mob forced Butman to come out, where the kidnapper barely escaped with his life before being run out of town.[45]

As a strategy, mobbing risked violence but also could prove remarkably effective at reasserting the meaning of freedom. Yet, African Americans used other tactics to thwart kidnapping and recapture, including forging freedom papers. If kidnappers could easily forge receipts for the purchase of "slaves," blacks could also craft documents that staked claims to citizenship. As vital as the documents were, it is surprising that scholars have paid them so little attention: a piece of paper that might be damaged, lost, or stolen could literally mean the difference between slavery and freedom. With the help of literate blacks and sympathetic whites, African Americans forged free papers. Slave owners complained that "despicable characters" were helping slaves escape "by furnishing them with tickets [for travel] in their master's names."[46] The practice was common enough that Kentucky passed laws specifically against falsifying travel passes and certificates of freedom. In one Kentucky fugitive slave case, Judge Walker Reid reminded a grand jury that laws prohibited the "making or furnishing, a forged pass, of freedom, or any other forged paper" to aid the self-emancipated.[47] So African Americans, often with the aid of white northern allies, devised their own strategies to combat kidnappers' tactics. Such strategies could prove highly effective, if perilous, and they highlight the role that black northerners themselves played in the long, undulating story of American freedom.

As they continued to battle kidnappers and slave catchers in their communities, northern African American intellectuals like Loguen maintained their fight against those who provided religious and legal cover for the Fugitive Slave Law. In response to an 1856 pro-Union sermon by the Reverend H. Mattison, Loguen criticized Mattison and other moderate northerners who detested slavery and even despised the recently passed Fugitive Slave Act but nonetheless advocated obedience to the law. Such obedience, Loguen charged, is "positively criminal not only—*it is cowardly.*" Like black and white abolitionists elsewhere, Loguen maintained that conscience and a commitment to the law of God rather than of man necessitated active resistance to the law. God's law was preeminent over any earthly ruler, Loguen declared, "be he Augustus, Pilate, or Franklin Pierce."[48]

During the decades between 1830 and 1850, pitched battles between free-soil and proslavery forces over the meaning of state borders lay at the heart of the sectional crisis, but the Fugitive Slave Law that passed as part of the compromise measures in 1850 made that crisis certain, providing the veneer of legality to kidnapping, since little proof was required to claim a free African American was a runaway.[49] The 1850 Fugitive Slave Law, designed to recover runaways, aided kidnappers of free blacks.

Kidnapping was risky for white criminals, not only because free blacks might be armed and ready to defend their families but also because northern governors resented the embarrassing ease with which their borders were violated. Such opposition was easily overcome with forged papers buttressed by bought white testimony. Claiming that a free black was actually your runaway slave could now net a trader a healthy profit, with the flimsy imprimatur of a formal legal process. Because northern courts often refused to recognize black testimony, whites could and did falsely claim free people who might have lost or had stolen their freedom papers.[50]

If the conflict that would become the Civil War began in the 1820s, it had reached epic proportions by the fall of 1850.[51] It was open season, it seemed, on free people, who could be turned into money overnight. "The act had scarcely become the law of the land," according to one historian, "when some parts of Indiana began to be overrun by man-hunters."[52] African Americans fled northern and midwestern cities like Indianapolis and Pittsburgh, hoping to reach Canada before being kidnapped or recaptured.[53] New reigns of terror opened up in northern communities as even callow kidnappers and slave catchers, emboldened by the new Fugitive Slave Act, believed they could arrest and capture African Americans with impunity and rely on northern officials and juries to step aside and willingly uphold the return of "runaways," whether they were really fugitives or not.

Despite having the odds further stacked against them by the new law, African Americans pressed courts and political leaders time and again to recognize their humanity and right to liberty. Court petition records tell us much about the struggles of free persons of color to stake assertions of liberty, and so too do they reflect the ease with which white southerners reached into "free soil" to lay claim to supposed runaways, often with the complicity of white northern officials, rendering slavery a national institution long before the *Dred Scott* case in 1857. But the reach of planter power into northern free soil did not go unchallenged, and the vigorous protests by antislavery activists threatened to cleave northern communities embroiled in an internal struggle over the meaning of slavery and free soil.

Northerners reacted so strongly against the law in part because they saw it as a violation of states' rights.[54] The Fugitive Slave Act, a pro-Union Philadelphian complained, "[had] transferred the seat of nullification from Charleston to Boston."[55] A Unionist New Yorker agreed: "From whence comes the cry of nullification now? . . . From the North!"[56] The law, many northerners cried, brought slavery to their doorstep, forcing them to become complicit in the rendition of suspected runaways. Free-soil judges, local officials, city jails, and courtrooms would all now play roles in protecting southern slavery. For many this was an untenable violation of states' rights, and they debated openly whether or not to obey the law.

Free-soil denunciation of the Fugitive Slave Law marked a crucial shift in northern and midwestern ideology. In making the case for a law higher than the Constitution, political leaders like Seward were openly acknowledging what white southerners and northern Unionists had been claiming for a generation at least: many free-state Americans had come to view the Constitution as a deeply flawed document. Northern and midwestern whites rejected significant parts of the nation's founding document; by the fall of 1850 they had come to see the Constitution's compromise over slavery, that precariously built wall between bondage and freedom erected in 1787, as a wall no longer worth propping up.

As the fugitive slave crisis erupted in the 1840s and 1850s, as free-soil citizens angrily denounced the violation of their states' rights, they came to view both the Union and its governing blueprint as fatally flawed. The Fugitive Slave Law had clarified all, and beginning in the fall of 1850, the debate over law and slavery was as loud and boisterous as any debate had been over any issue since the nation's founding. New England preacher Kazlitt Arvine predicted, "In every legislature, in every court and college and debating room and public house, on every rail-car and steamboat, in thousands of reviews and news-prints, and in many a pulpit too, this bill of infamy will be discussed, and the hatred of slavery and pity for the slave be deepened."[57] Despite the combined efforts of Unionists in and out of Washington to render the law a "final settlement" on slavery, Arvine proved prescient. Throughout the 1850s, the crises over fugitive slaves, northern states' rights, and the validity of the constitutional compromise over slavery would continue unabated.

Famed abolitionist William Cooper Nell was an important member of Boston's black community and a leading opponent of the kidnapping of African Americans. (Wikimedia)

This 1850 print published after the passage of the Fugitive Slave Law illustrated the ways in which the legislation was antithetical to the Bible and the Declaration of Independence. (Theodor Kaufmann, *Effects of the Fugitive-Slave-Law* [New York: Hoff & Bloede, 1850]; Library of Congress)

This illustration depicts Philadelphia abolitionists protecting Jane Johnson and her children from the clutches of John Wheeler. (From William Still's 1872 book *The Underground Railroad*; Wikimedia)

Jane Johnson became a heroine for Philadelphia's black community. A plaque celebrating her escape sits along the Delaware River. (From William Still's 1872 book *The Underground Railroad*; Wikimedia)

CAUTION!!
COLORED PEOPLE
OF BOSTON, ONE & ALL,

You are hereby respectfully CAUTIONED and advised, to avoid conversing with the

Watchmen and Police Officers of Boston,

For since the recent ORDER OF THE MAYOR & ALDERMEN, they are empowered to act as

KIDNAPPERS
AND
Slave Catchers,

And they have already been actually employed in KIDNAPPING, CATCHING, AND KEEPING SLAVES. Therefore, if you value your LIBERTY, and the *Welfare of the Fugitives* among you, *Shun* them in every possible manner, as so many *HOUNDS* on the track of the most unfortunate of your race.

Keep a Sharp Look Out for KIDNAPPERS, and have TOP EYE open.

APRIL 24, 1851.

Broadsides and flyers such as this one posted in Boston in 1851 warned African Americans when slavecatchers were spotted. (Library of Congress)

The Anthony Burns case in 1854 shocked Massachusetts residents as well as citizens across the free states. (Boston Public Library, Rare Books Department)

The case of George Latimer convinced many in and around Boston that northern free-soil states had to fight for their rights as states. (Massachusetts Historical Society)

PROCEEDINGS

OF THE

STATE

DISUNION CONVENTION;

HELD AT

WORCESTER, MASSACHUSETTS,

JANUARY 15, 1857.

PHONOGRAPHICALLY REPORTED BY J. M. W. YERRINTON.

BOSTON:
PRINTED FOR THE COMMITTEE.
1857.

The emergence of a powerful states' rights ideology in free states indicated that free-soilers had become impatient with the Constitution's compromise over slavery. (Archive.org)

Although the Constitutional Union Party, led in the 1860 presidential election by candidates John Bell and Edward Everett, garnered some support in Upper South states such as Tennessee, there was little support for a middle-of-the-road position on slavery in the free states. (Library of Congress)

ANTI-SLAVERY MASS MEETING!

Agreeably to a call, signed by about 50 persons, and published in the Lawrence Republican, a Mass Meeting of the friends of Freedom will be held at Miller's Hall, at 2 o'clock P. M., on Friday, Dec. 2d the day on which

CAPT. JOHN BROWN IS TO BE EXECUTED,

To testify against the iniquitous SLAVE POWER that rules this Nation, and take steps to

Organize the Anti-Slavery Sentiment

of the community. Arrangements have been made with prominent speakers to be present and address the meeting.
PER ORDER OF COMMITTEE OF ARRANGEMENTS.
Lawrence, Nov. 26, 1859.

Though abolitionists in the mid-Atlantic and Northeast attracted considerable attention, the abolitionist movement stretched along the western reaches of the border between free and slave states. (Kansas Historical Society)

CHAPTER FOUR

Trying to Save the Union

Battles over the Fugitive Slave Law in the 1850s

As free-state citizens erupted over the legitimacy of the Fugitive Slave Act in the latter months of 1850 and early 1851, the federal government moved swiftly to demonstrate its resolve to enforce the law. Some historians who have studied the 1850s, such as Michael Holt and David Potter, have argued that the passage of the act, as well as Washington's commitment to enforcing the law, created a lull in the turmoil over fugitive slaves.[1] I have found no such hiatus. In fact, throughout the 1850s, battles erupted repeatedly over self-emancipation, the rights of northern states to keep slavery out of their borders, and the increasing unwillingness of northerners to participate in fugitive renditions.

It is true that political leaders in support of the compromise measures clearly made a pact: they would send federal marshals with the cooperation of local authorities into every major northern and midwestern metropolis, from Chicago to New York, to make high-profile arrests of suspected runaways.[2] In Boston, William and Ellen Craft became the visible targets, while officials in New York City arrested James Hamlet, and Henry Garnett was taken into custody in Philadelphia, all to show northerners that state and local laws would be trumped by a federal government committed to upholding the constitutional compromise between slavery and freedom, and specifically the new law on runaways.

As federal officials tried to provide examples of their determination to enforce the compromise, the country's black population wondered if they would be sacrificed to save the Union. The interstate crisis over kidnapping and fugitive slaves, already decades old by 1861, told African Americans that northern whites were often willing allies of southern planters. While the danger of kidnapping was great, and the hegemony of Unionism strong enough to underpin white law-breaking in hundreds of cases, blacks and whites defied that hegemony with tactics of their own. Just as in the antebellum South, in which the planter hegemony faced constant challenges from a burgeoning white middle class that resented planter power and wealth, so too did the northern Unionist hegemony face threats to its considerable power.[3] As we have seen, African Americans and their northern white allies combated conservative Unionism by forging freedom papers, warning fellow African Americans of man stealers in their midst, and mobbing to rescue the recaptured or kidnapped.

Just as the anger over the Fugitive Slave Law fueled a reassessment among white northerners regarding the feasibility and desirability of preserving the Union, so too did the law reshape African American intellectual and political culture. By the late 1840s, despite the persistence of emigration activists, African Americans had spent decades fighting racial exclusion and colonization schemes. In 1849, black leader James W. C. Pennington angrily denounced emigration and colonization in New York City.[4] In fact, as historian Benjamin Quarles pointed out several years ago, black opposition to colonization helped convince white abolitionists, including William Lloyd Garrison, that colonization was an insidious form of racism and dehumanization. Garrison's tract *Thoughts on African Colonization* made the case against emigration and set the tone for northern white abolitionists.[5]

But the devastating surprise of the Fugitive Slave Law led to an immediate and sustained reexamination of emigration. In the fall of 1850, shortly after word of the law filtered into northern black communities, thousands of African Americans fled Pittsburgh, Detroit, New York, and other cities. Most went to Canada, but others took to Mexico or the Caribbean. African Americans who remained debated staying in the United States, believing with good reason that the interests of African Americans had once again been sacrificed in hopes of saving the feeble, tattered Union. Martin Delany, for example, who had long opposed colonization, wrote in 1852 that the Fugitive Slave Law had forced blacks to reconsider emigration.[6] And as historian Patrick Rael has argued, the Fugitive Slave Law led many African Americans to reconsider the wisdom of integration even if blacks did stay in the United States. At an 1853 convention black leaders led unprecedented calls for separate black schools.[7]

Many African Americans reacted to the Fugitive Slave Law with calls for racial exclusiveness and emigration, but just as many African Americans newly resolved to fight the law, with violence if necessary. "It is true," African American leader Thomas Scott remarked to the Convention of the Colored Citizens in Gallia County, Ohio, in 1851, "that the start of our hope has been hid in obscurity behind the dark cloud of the Fugitive Slave Bill, yet I believe if we labor with unwearied diligence, the victory will be ours."[8] Important works on African American resistance and the origins of the Black Power movement have focused on the mid-twentieth century, but the history of resistance and assertion of black power dates to far earlier. In response to the Fugitive Slave Law, African Americans armed themselves, formed vigilance committees to defend against abduction, and organized networks to warn when slave hunters appeared.[9] The African American state convention in Albany in July 1851 pledged to thwart any attempts by compromising white politicians to take away their "dearest rights and liberties, belonging to us as freemen."[10] Elaborate alarm systems emerged in Syracuse, Rochester, and Christiana, Pennsylvania.[11] Born a slave in Richmond, William P. Newman escaped and settled in Ohio. When word of the Fugitive Slave Law spread, Newman vowed "to kill any so-called man who attempts to enslave me or mine, if possible, though it be Millard Fillmore himself."[12] African Americans throughout the North and West pledged to defend themselves and their families from slave hunters and openly embraced an ideology that stressed the legitimacy of using violence in the face of capture. A new and potent rhetoric based on armed resistance reverberated throughout the black community in the wake of the passage of the Fugitive Slave Law.[13]

The Fugitive Slave Law led both white and black northerners to reassess and reformulate long-held ideologies, but it was the peculiar cycle in which the Fugitive Slave Law played out that caused repeated damage to the cause of those who would maintain the Union. When a suspected runaway was seized in the North, either by slave hunters from the South or by northern officials themselves, an outcry of anger among blacks and whites erupted—driven by a combination of righteous anger over the violation of states' rights and humanitarian concern for the accused runaway—and caused riots, angry rallies, and sometimes the violent seizure of the accused from the clutches of the authorities.[14] As the telegraph spread news of northern recalcitrance, white southerners reacted with equal venom, claiming that northerners abrogated the constitutional compact. In this case the southerners were right; that's exactly what northern activists were doing. Black and white northerners, some of whom were longtime devotees of the abolitionist cause and others who were new converts to the antislavery movement driven by the Fugitive Slave Law, readily acknowledged that they adhered to a "higher law" and staked their claim on grounds that began as religious and humanitarian sentiments and quickly becoming politicized. As Carl Schurz realized with hindsight in the late nineteenth century, this cycle of action and reaction repeated itself throughout the 1850s. The repeated refusal to enforce the Fugitive Slave Law, Schurz pointed out, "would increase the exasperation of the slave-holders by its failure, while exasperating the people of the Free States by the attempts at enforcement. Thus the compromise of 1850, instead of securing peace and harmony, contained in the most important of its provisions the seeds of new and greater conflicts."[15]

Those seeds took root as soon as the Fugitive Slave Law became public. In New York in October 1850, just weeks after President Fillmore signed the law, James Hamlet was seized and returned to southern slaveholders, followed by the well-publicized escape of William and Ellen Craft. The following February, slave hunters working undercover seized runaway Shadrach Minkins from his job as a waiter in a Boston coffeehouse; as word spread, a furious biracial mob surrounded the Boston courthouse, broke in, and hurriedly escorted a stunned Minkins into the Underground Railroad, which ultimately carried him to permanent freedom in Canada. Similar incidents erupted throughout the Midwest and Northeast in the 1850s. The seizure of Thomas Sims in the spring of 1851 and of Anthony Burns in 1854, and the return of both to slavery, radicalized northern opinion. African American activist Jermain Wesley Loguen wrote to Frederick Douglass of a successful abolitionist speaking tour in the summer after the Fugitive Slave Law: "We found many and true friends on the way, that have been made so by the wicked Fugitive Slave Bill. . . . I never had a better hearing."[16] And, as Schurz argued later in the century, northern resentment over the violation of state laws prohibiting the seizure of runaways helped convince many northerners—especially Whigs, but even many Democrats—that no legitimate Union could be maintained with slaveholders and the Washington politicians they controlled. Schurz asserted, "An outcry arose, not only from colored people and anti-slavery men, but from persons who, although they had so far taken little interest in the matter, now felt their human sympathies and their moral sense insulted by the things they witnessed among themselves. The anti-slavery men took advantage of this change of feeling, and meetings were held in Northern cities ringing with denunciations of the fugitive-slave law."[17]

For white southerners, northerners' open refusal to obey the Fugitive Slave Law only added further weight to fire-eater claims of the impossibility of a constitutional union with the free states. In response to Bostonians' anger over the capture of Shadrach Minkins and Thomas Sims, citizens in New Bern, North Carolina, met and drafted a series of resolutions, pledging that they would not trade with those who refused to abide by the law.[18] Georgia legislators officially chastised northerners for disobeying the law and used the dispute to reiterate calls for secession. Each time white southerners read in their newspapers and magazines about a spoiled attempt to recapture a runaway, southern anger intensified; in fact, some claimed that extradition of fugitives under an independent southern state would be easier than sending furtive slave catchers into northern towns. Speaking of northern refusal to send back runaways, North Carolina congressman David Outlaw claimed, "[It] furnishes more material for agitation than anything else, because it is a practical evil which we suffer, and a palpable wrong which the North commits."[19] In language that might easily have been uttered by northern opponents of the corrupt bargain of 1850, South Carolina's Langdon Cheves scorned even the word "compromise." He attacked "the dastard who would have consented to accept compromises, or talk of taking a fragment of those rights as 'the best we could get.'"[20] It is telling that abolitionists and secessionists jumped on the Compromise of 1850 and the Fugitive Slave Law as evidence that compromise itself was a dirty word. Extremists in both sections recognized an opportunity to discredit moderates.

What did northern opposition to the Fugitive Slave Law look like in practice? It is one matter to oppose a law in speeches and sermons; it is quite another to engage in outright and active defiance of the law. Yet, as the cases of Shadrach Minkins, William Parker, and Joshua Glover demonstrate, black and white activists were willing to venture beyond words.

The Minkins Affair

Richard Henry Dana was the last person one would expect to become embroiled in the fight to defend runaways like Shadrach Minkins. By the time he reached his mid-twenties, Dana had already earned fame and fortune. From the time his mother swaddled him in the fine English linens cherished by Boston's elite, Dana seemed destined for a comfortable life as an author and New England aristocrat. After all, Dana's ancestors had helped settle Massachusetts Bay Colony in the 1630s, and Dana's literary father knew Boston's wealthy literati personally. Dana himself cut his literary teeth around the family dinner table, which counted among its guests Washington Irving, William Cullen Bryant, and Henry Wadsworth Longfellow. The Dana family maintained close ties to the incestuous world of Cambridge, and Harvard was as much a part of the family history as the clan's colonial legacy. Though the Danas did not always live in complete luxury devoid of financial worries, their name alone secured a life of leisure.

Richard Dana, however, was not interested in merely coasting through a life of aristocratic ease. He was proud of his family's heritage, but he determined early not to be bound by the chains of the past. Rejecting the usual path of adventure for the New England elite, the well-worn Grand Tour of Europe's capital cities, Dana decided at just nineteen years old to embark on a journey completely at odds with his comfortable upbringing. For nearly twenty-four months, Dana experienced the decidedly unaristocratic life of a sailor, joining a crew in its mission to round Cape Horn and gather trading goods along the western coast of South and Central America. Dana would later chronicle his journey in *Two Years before the Mast*, an instant classic that landed him immediate and lasting fame as an American author. The tale's success stunned both Dana and his publisher, almost single-handedly reviving the fortunes of Harper Brothers. Still in his mid-twenties when the book became a best seller in 1841, Dana, with an early receding hairline and short, stocky frame, entered Harvard to study law. Although he would go on to a distinguished law career, by his own admission he reached the pinnacle of his fame at the young age of twenty-five.

Fortunately for Shadrach Minkins and other fugitive slaves, however, Dana refused to rest on his literary fame. In fact, perhaps even to the great surprise of Dana himself, the young lawyer became one of the great heroes of the fight over runaways in Boston. At great personal risk, Dana boldly and persistently defended numerous former slaves in the 1850s. His antislavery fervor, which included a close alliance with the Free-Soil Party, became grounds for the scorn of family and now former friends. Boston's leading aristocrat George Ticknor penned a letter to Dana dissolving their formerly close friendship and promising never to speak to him again. Despite the personal hurt and the loss of professional reputation, Dana pressed on in defending not just Shadrach but other celebrated cases of runaways in and around Boston.

Dana first caught wind of the Shadrach case within a few hours of the capture on February 15, 1851. Given his connections to the legal authorities in Boston, Dana quickly ascertained the dramatic circumstances surrounding the runaway's seizure at Taft's Coffeehouse. Shadrach's customers that morning in February included two white men, hardly unusual breakfast clientele for the coffeehouse. The day, however, turned out to be far from routine. On this day, at this table, Shadrach experienced his most-dreaded nightmare. The two breakfasting men, one a deputy marshal and the other a former constable, arrested Minkins for being a runaway and quickly ferried him to the courthouse. So shocked was Shadrach at his arrest, and so rushed was he from the coffeehouse, that he didn't even have time to remove his apron.

Dana ran immediately to the courthouse. There he found the judge and court officials in place, and "a good looking black fellow" seated at the defense table. Dana was surprised that few other people had heard of the capture. "The arrest had been so sudden & unexpected," Dana wrote in his diary, "that few knew it, & it was half an hour before the crowd assembled, but it was increasing every minute & there was great excitement."[21] Word of Minkins's arrest spread quickly within Boston's African American community, which numbered several hundred in 1851. It should not have been a surprise, therefore, when ordinary African Americans took the matter of Shadrach's arrest and his possible return to slavery in Virginia into their own hands.

Word of Shadrach's seizure crashed upon the shores of Boston's black community, and shortly after his arrest, more than one hundred black men had gathered outside the courthouse. Inside, five abolitionist lawyers, including Dana and prominent African American Robert Morris, succeeded in adjourning the case so that they could prepare Shadrach's defense. Dana returned to his office across the street from the courthouse. But at noon African Americans who had gathered outside burst through the courtroom door and, to the shock of all present, including Minkins himself, seized the runaway. The few stunned guards merely stood by as dozens of African Americans rushed Shadrach out the courthouse's back door. Before the stupefied judge and lawyers, the mob whisked Shadrach away into the streets of Boston. Dana had just returned to his office when he heard shouts coming from inside the courthouse. Peering out his window, Dana saw "two huge negroes" descending the courthouse steps: "[They bore] the prisoner between them, with his clothes half torn off, & so stupefied by the sudden rescue & the violence of his dragging off that he sat almost down, & I thought had fainted." Soon Minkins had regained his feet, and "they went off toward Cambridge, like a black squall, the crowd driving along with them & cheering as they went."[22]

No one was harmed in the melee, but according to legend the emboldened black mob paused briefly to remember Crispus Attucks, a mixed-race victim of the Boston Massacre and a freedom-fighting symbol of American independence. Minkins hid in the Beacon Hill attic of Lewis Hayden, a prominent black businessman known for ferrying runaways along the Underground Railroad. Boston's police and federal marshals tried to pursue the fast-moving throng, but as if acting with one mind, the African American crowd shielded Shadrach from view and quickly disappeared into a black neighborhood. During the night, amidst a powerful storm, as if nature had sent rainfall to wash away the taint of slavery from an anxious Shadrach once and for all, the runaway hid in Hayden's attic. With the aid of the Underground Railroad, Minkins escaped to Canada and joined other former slaves now living in freedom and no longer fearing the slave hunter's steps.

Dana had barely time enough to begin Shadrach's defense when the opportunity to strike a legal blow to the Fugitive Slave Law vanished with the black crowd that seized Minkins. But Dana's commitment to proving the law immoral and unconstitutional endured, and in 1854 he defended another runaway, Anthony Burns. This time Dana was able to see the trial to the end, and though he lost the case, Dana's performance as Burns's defender added legal renown to his literary fame. Dana, the offspring of old wealthy Boston, a man who could easily have rested on the reputation garnered by the popularity of *Two Years before the Mast*, had chosen a different life, one that would earn him respect not just from the Lowells, Longfellows, and Emersons but also from the most powerless and vulnerable Bostonians, the runaways yearning for freedom.

Dana, like many Bostonians white and black, feared and distrusted the slave hunters who furtively slipped into free cities like spies from another country. A caricature of such hunters formed in the minds of northerners, and vigilance committees kept a careful eye for the tell-tale characteristics: a mean, angry demeanor, an ugly countenance, and a tendency to drink and swear in public. At one trial Dana himself remarked on the appearance of slave catchers: "More despicable wretches in appearance than the Southern agents I never beheld—cruel, low-bred, dissolute, degraded beings! No man's life or property would be safe a moment in their hands."[23] Dana was right in an important regard: most slave hunters were lower-class whites who hoped to supplement their meager incomes by chasing after runaways, often alongside bloodhounds specially bred to hunt down fugitives. Slaves tried to throw off the dogs by sprinkling pepper or other spices on the trail. Hunters could earn as much as fifty dollars for bringing back a slave, in addition to expenses. It was a lucrative but dangerous business. Desperate runaways had little to lose in fighting off slave catchers.[24]

To those who had the misfortune to meet him in person, John Caphart seemed ideally suited to the role of slave catcher. Hundreds of southern men made their living as bounty hunters, paid to track runaway slaves and return them to bondage, by force if necessary. Officially, Caphart earned a living as a constable in Norfolk, but he had his dirtied hands in a range of unpleasant enterprises, from operating a private jail to slave trading to debt collection. But Caphart himself remarked, "I am often employed by private persons to pursue fugitive slaves [and] I never refuse a good job of that kind."[25] A former seaman, Caphart once beat a man nearly to death and claimed that the victim's "rudest and most insulting manner" demanded it. Back in Virginia, Caphart earned fifty cents for each slave he whipped at the request of a master who could not stomach the task. In 1851, the sixty-year-old Caphart was charged with illegally kidnapping Shadrach Minkins in the heart of the abolitionist lions' den. Slave hunters like Caphart employed a range of illicit tactics to identify the location of runaways. Yet Boston was a logical place to begin, given the city's well-earned reputation for harboring runaways.

Caphart's appearance and demeanor immediately set him apart in Boston, where white and black citizens became suspicious. Like many bounty hunters who ventured into northern cities, Caphart pretended to be a businessman on a buying trip, roving from storefront to storefront, lurking in bars and hotels, gathering information at each stop. Abolitionists later remarked how well Caphart fit the devilish, mean looks of a kidnapper. "He is a thin, tall fellow," one observer noted, "rather lean and lanky" with "an uncommonly hard, bad face, and ugly, not only in form and feature, but expression,—a face which seems made for a slave hunter, or by his business." According to Dana, Caphart had "a restless dark eye, and an anxious careworn look."[26] Caphart was so infamous among northerners that he became the model for Harriet Beecher Stowe's depiction of slave catchers in *Uncle Tom's Cabin*.

Slave owners employed hunters like Caphart in hopes of recapturing a lost slave or at least partially recouping a slave's value. From birth, white children were told of the inherent inferiority of African Americans through a pervasive proslavery ideology. "Let any man who questions" whether blacks are better off under slavery, a Georgian claimed in a typically racist rant, go to Africa himself "and compare the Negro trained under the influences of slavery with the Negro of the same generation reared in his native barbarism."[27] Whites were so convinced of their slaves' contentment that they were surprised when slaves ran away. Decades of instruction had told white owners that their bondspeople were naturally childlike and relished the master's protection. When slaves did abscond, many owners believed that their slaves had been coaxed into fleeing by trouble-making free blacks or meddlesome abolitionists. Whites believed their own propaganda that once found runaways would readily admit their mistake in escaping and beg for forgiveness. Masters could not fathom that blacks really did yearn for freedom with the same commitment and intensity as whites.

Christiana

Edward Gorsuch was one such slave owner. Like many plantation farmers near the Mason-Dixon Line, Gorsuch took repeated financial hits from slaves who ran away. Given that slaves were expensive, worth in modern terms upwards of $15,000 or more, Gorsuch and other masters worked hard to recapture what they considered their property. When four of his slaves fled in 1849, Gorsuch determined to locate and regain his property. The four runaways settled near the home of another escaped slave, William Parker. Parker had settled in Christiana, Pennsylvania, among free blacks, one of whom tipped off Gorsuch in hopes of reward. In September 1851, just months after Shadrach Minkins's ordeal, Gorsuch and several men including his son crossed the border into Pennsylvania fiercely resolute in finding his property.

Parker learned of the impending invasion, and even though he was not Gorsuch's property, Parker became embroiled in the deadly fight that followed. Parker knew all too well what it was like to be pursued by slave catchers. "It was whispered about that the slaveholders intended to make an attack on my house," Parker recalled. "The bloodhounds were on my track." Parker and local fugitives had already established a secretive association for their mutual protection, promising to sound a horn if hunters came to their doorstep. So when Gorsuch and his posse approached Parker's Pennsylvania home, a neighbor sounded the alarm by blowing a horn, bringing black protestors as well as white abolitionists to the scene. Other runaways gathered in the second floor of Parker's home, armed with guns. Parker was determined to die before being returned to bondage; Gorsuch was equally set on retaking his property and had brought the local U.S. marshal to help.

Gorsuch employed a tactic common in such affairs, asking the runaways, who were holed up in the second floor of Parker's house, "Ain't I always treated you fairly? . . . Didn't I always feed and clothe you well and not whip you unless'n you deserved it?" To Gorsuch, as long as his property had been taken care of adequately, there was no cause for complaint. He failed to grasp the ex-slaves' desire for liberty. Twenty-six-year-old Abraham Johnson, who had also run away from Gorsuch's plantation, denied the legitimacy of chattel bondage: "Does such a shriveled up old slaveholder as you," Johnson taunted from the second floor window, "own such a nice, genteel young man as I am?" Johnson's taunting hit its target, and Gorsuch angrily announced he was coming up to the second floor with the marshal to round up his slaves. As Gorsuch warned Parker, "You had better give up . . . and come down, for I have come a long way this morning and want my breakfast; for my property I will have, or I'll breakfast in hell."[28] Gorsuch got his wish. In the melee that followed, he was shot and killed.

Though Gorsuch's actual killer remains unclear, Parker knew he would be blamed, and he fled by foot toward Philadelphia. White Quakers and black country folks helped Parker escape detection, allowing him to sleep in barns and serving him food, but Parker soon heard that officials were looking for him in Philadelphia: "I learned from a preacher, directly from the city, that the excitement in Philadelphia was too great for us to risk our safety by going there." After meandering in the countryside near the city, Parker decided to board a train in Philadelphia to go to Frederick Douglass's home in Rochester, New York. Parker and a fellow fugitive snuck into town, grabbed dust from a nearby brickyard and smeared it over the clothes, and posed as city brick workers. Douglass, whose home became known among African Americans as an important stop on the Underground Railroad, helped Parker cross into Canada. "We landed at Kingston on the 21st of September," Parker later wrote, "at six o'clock in the morning, and walked around for a long time, without meeting anyone we had ever known." But Parker had reached a region known for welcoming runaways, and soon after arriving in Canada he even began publishing articles in abolitionist newspapers. Parker's wife and children eventually joined him and they lived free in Canada. "[After] a struggle of many years," Parker proclaimed, "[I have] settled upon British soil, [and] realized fully the grandeur of my position as a free man." Were Gorsuch and his slave catchers around to read Parker's words, they might have finally understood that all the food and clothing in the world could not replace a searing hunger for liberty.

The federal government's resolve was tested in one of the more captivating fugitive slave stories from the Midwest. Joshua Glover escaped slavery in St. Louis in 1852 and made his way to Racine, Wisconsin, realizing that if he were ever discovered he would be closer to freedom in Canada. Glover lived for two years in Racine, earning respect in the small frontier town for his hard work and character. But in 1854 agents of Glover's former master tracked him down after slinking around town and asking questions. They subdued the panicked Glover and with the help of local officials jailed him in Milwaukee. Wisconsin was already a hotbed of antislavery sentiment, and the controversy over the Glover incident would help convince residents to form the Republican Party. Glover's white and black neighbors, incensed by the "kidnapping" of one of their own, boarded the next ship to Milwaukee.

Glover escaped in no small part because of the large protests erupting in Milwaukee after his arrest. Glover received the support of newspaper editor and antislavery activist Sherman Booth, who led a mob of about five thousand protestors soon after word had spread of the runaway's recapture. Booth and his accomplices were to pay dearly for their actions, since the federal government was determined to enforce the Fugitive Slave Law. In the eyes of Unionists, everything was riding on the successful execution of a law designed to uphold the constitutional compromise over slavery.[29]

Intrastate Conflict before the Civil War

The most significant consequence of the Glover affair was a bold and highly controversial decision by the Wisconsin Supreme Court that thundered across the nation. In attempting to prosecute the white abolitionists who aided Glover's escape, the federal government had charged Booth with treason for violating the Fugitive Slave Law. The Wisconsin court declared, in one of the most profound iterations of free states' rights to emerge in the entire antebellum era, that the federal runaway law violated Wisconsin's authority to determine the status of people within its borders. The Fugitive Slave Law, therefore, in a decision that echoed the South Carolina nullification movement more than twenty years prior, was unenforceable within Wisconsin.

To abolitionists, it seemed perfectly reasonable to appropriate southern states' rights doctrines. "If Massachusetts had the right and the power to abolish slavery in 1780," *The Liberator* asked, "where is the power that can be rightfully exercised, which can 'command' her to aid and assist in establishing and perpetuating the same 'accursed institution'"?[30] The answer was that white southerners viewed states' rights only as a means to protect and extend slavery. As the antislavery *National Era* newspaper angrily argued, southerners believed "in State rights for the South, but not for the North."[31] In fact, if every state had an independent court immune from overrule by the U.S. Supreme Court, Wisconsin wanted the right to declare the Fugitive Slave Law unconstitutional. The result, Unionists declared, would be chaos and an unraveling of the national compromise. "The annunciation of the doctrine that the State courts are not bound by the decisions of the Supreme Courts of the United States," the *Louisville Journal* maintained, ". . . is calculated to create a mischievous feeling of hostility to that valuable part of our National Constitution."[32] That was quite an understatement. In fact, the Fugitive Slave Law, the worsening of interstate conflict as the fury over Kansas and its status as a free or slave state boiled over, and the failure of popular sovereignty together prompted a new movement to repeal the Fugitive Slave Law.

In the sweltering Washington summer of 1854, lawmakers gathered to confront the fact that the Fugitive Slave Law passed in 1850 was a miserable failure. Far from resolving or even remotely quieting the sectional crisis, the law had managed to increase both northern *and* southern fury. Northerners were becoming indignant at a law that seemed to violate their rights to outlaw slavery within their state borders, while white southern fire-eaters pointed to free-state intransigence and abolitionist propaganda as proof that the Union was doomed. In late August, the Senate began debating the notion of repealing the law at the behest of Sumner, who had argued for repeal not long after the law was signed in September 1850. Southern senators tried to stop Sumner's motion for repeal, but free-state senators wanted a hearing.[33] Seeking to influence free-state senators to vote in favor of repeal, more than two dozen women abolitionists, including Maria Weston Chapman, Eliza Lee Follen, and Caroline Weston, signed a petition in favor of repeal.[34]

To boost these efforts, northerners continued their denunciations of the law in state legislatures. Pennsylvania free-soil Democrats deplored the law, resolving, "It legalizes injustice, promotes domestic turmoil, weakens our power for common defense [and] promotes general discontent." The lawmakers called for its immediate repeal.[35] Late in 1854, Vermont state legislators contributed to a new wave of personal liberty and antikidnapping laws by making slave renditions more difficult. In addition to imposing a heavy fine of $3,000 for falsely claiming a slave, the act required at least two credible witnesses to support a slaveholder's claim and reaffirmed habeas corpus guarantees that were absent from the federal law.[36]

Just how far northern opinion had shifted away from compromise became evident when Senator Stephen Douglas came to Chicago in the fall of 1854. Just four years before, he successfully defended the Compromise of 1850 against abolitionist attacks, reassuring the city council that the Fugitive Slave Law merely reaffirmed existing constitutional law and did not represent a new or alarming burden on the free states. Now, after having supported the failed popular sovereignty movements in Kansas and Nebraska, Douglas was met with "groans and hisses" so loud that he could not finish a speech in North

Market Hall.[37] Almost exactly four years after his powerful and convincing defense of the Fugitive Slave Law quieted dissent, Douglas was not even allowed to offer his reasons for supporting compromise with the South over slavery. Douglas was discovering that just as the South had formulated a regional identity, the North had similarly coalesced around a set of free-state principles that elevated conscience and northern states' rights above the need to enforce the constitutional compromise over slavery. Before he died, Daniel Webster had declared, "There is no North." Now, abolitionists and an increasing number of northerners were creating one. "Mr. Webster was mistaken," *The Liberator* avowed in 1854. "There is a North; but the instinctive, strong, conscientious love of liberty, felt by the North, finds but feeble and imperfect expression through the politicians or public men."[38] Although Garrison remained dubious about the sincerity of free-state politicians across the country, he understood that the crisis over self-emancipation had awoken free-state citizens, including many who had never cared much about blacks or slavery. The repeated use of federal authority to invade free-state borders in the pursuit of runaways, the perception that every so-called compromise seemed to acquiesce to the interests of slaveholders, and the equally powerful conclusion many free-state voters had reached—that is, that the Constitution's compromises over slavery were no longer valid—all combined to represent a fundamental and dramatic shift in northern and western thinking regarding the Union and its future.

The West and the Fugitive Slave Crisis

As 1854 began, Congress once again found itself embroiled in controversy. The U.S. had already greatly expanded its holdings in the West as a result of the Mexican War and the Gadsden Purchase in late 1853, gaining territory that many free-state observers worried might become additions to the slavery empire. Even more ominous, Northern Democrats and southern leaders of all political stripes were eyeing Cuba and the Caribbean as possible new territories or states conducive to bondage.[39] Yet in January 1854, Congress was most immediately concerned with the Nebraska and Kansas Territories. Iowa Democratic senator Augustus Dodge had introduced a bill the previous month to organize the Nebraska Territory, a proposal that soon also included organizing Kansas. Southern politicians immediately became concerned that slavery would be prohibited unless the 36°30 line established by the Compromise of 1820 was erased. Antislavery politicians and voters were equally alarmed that an agreed-upon line that had been in effect for more than three decades was now in danger of repeal. Yet, with the help of the Doughface Democratic allies in Washington, southern politicians were successful in passing the Kansas-Nebraska Act in 1854.[40] Just as they had badly misjudged northern and western anger over the Fugitive Slave Law in 1850, so too did northern Democrats like Stephen Douglas misapprehend the fury over repealing the 1820 line. Indeed, free-state citizens were infuriated by another giveaway to the "slave power," a phrase that was appearing to more and more free-state residents as not mere political rhetoric but rather an authentic description of federal power and its repeated violation of free states' rights. Douglas especially was vilified across the North and West for his support of the Kansas-Nebraska Act. "I could travel from Boston to Chicago by the light of my own effigy," Douglas lamented. Even northern women got into the act, sending Douglas "thirty pieces of silver" in direct reference to the Biblical story of Judas's betrayal.[41]

While the Kansas-Nebraska fury might seem unrelated to the controversies over fugitive slaves, it is worth noting that the final text of the 1854 law indicated that runaways were very much at the forefront of congressmen's minds. In fact, right after establishing the basic governing structures for the territories, section 10 asserted that the 1793 and 1850 Fugitive Slave Laws were thereby "declared to extend to and be in full force within the limits of [the] Territory of Nebraska."[42] In fact, the western territories would witness nearly constant turmoil over runaways, controversies and tensions that the Kansas-Nebraska Act did almost nothing to quiet.

The Fugitive Slave Crisis, 1855–1856

The fact that cases were spread across the North, from Wisconsin and Iowa to Michigan and Indiana and throughout the Northeast, powerfully reminds modern readers that the sectional crisis did not just pit the Northeast against the Deep South but also incorporated passionate debates in the Midwest and West. The horrifying tale of Margaret Garner, who crossed the frozen Ohio River into freedom in the winter of 1856 only to be recaptured in her cousin's Cincinnati cabin, was perhaps the most publicized case of a female runaway. When she heard her master and his posse outside the cabin door, Garner panicked and killed one of her daughters with a knife rather than see that child returned to bondage. She would have killed her three other children as well if the white men had not busted down the door. In months of legal wrangling, court proceedings, and dramatic testimony, the case dragged on. Abolitionists sympathized with Garner and pointed to her actions as evidence of slavery's twisted influence. Proslavery forces counteracted that the killing demonstrated that blacks were inherently uncivilized and fit only for control under slavery.

The Glover and Garner cases incensed ordinary free-state citizens and even led some radical abolitionists to call for the free states to secede from the Union. With each passing year, the controversy over the recapture or rescue of runaways worsened. Although the Garner case is perhaps the best-known fugitive slave affair involving a female runaway, there were many others. When word spread that Garner had killed her child, abolitionists claimed that the incident proved slavery's devastating impact on women. The story of Jane Johnson's traumatic escape from slavery offered further proof in the minds of black and white northerners that slavery was an evil deserving of extinction.

As a slave owned by North Carolina diplomat John Wheeler, Jane Johnson had already suffered the horrifying trauma of watching one of her sons being sold away. Wheeler, who sported a bushy mustache that matched his graying hair and a thick southern accent, was a low-level but active Democratic politician. When Wheeler took Johnson and her two young sons with him to Philadelphia, en route to his new post as ambassador to Nicaragua via New York, Johnson and her sons escaped in a harrowing tale of desperation and courage. Although Wheeler had locked Johnson and her sons in their Philadelphia hotel room, with specific instructions not to talk to the all-black hotel staff, Johnson managed to inform a porter that she wanted to escape. The porter notified the local vigilance committee, a group of black and white abolitionists who offered protection to runaways. Word then spread to the Philadelphia Antislavery Society offices nearby, and a white abolitionist named Passmore Williamson met Wheeler, Johnson, and the young slave boys as they were about to board a ship to New York.

At the Philadelphia docks, Williamson told Wheeler that Johnson and her sons were now free under Philadelphia state law, and Williamson had brought with him five burly black dockworkers to restrain the loudly protesting Wheeler. William Still, a prominent African American abolitionist and member of the vigilance committee, quickly took Johnson and her sons to a waiting carriage and into hiding in the attic of his Philadelphia home. Ultimately Johnson and her sons settled in Boston with the help of suffragette Lucretia Mott, and until her death in 1872 Johnson relished the freedom she and her sons had won.

For the Philadelphia abolitionists who had arranged her escape, however, the aftermath of the rescue lingered. The diplomat Wheeler used his political influence to press his case, and Passmore Williamson and William Still were jailed for contempt for failing to divulge Johnson's whereabouts. John Kintzing Kane, a proslavery Philadelphia judge and prominent Democrat, kept Williamson in jail for more than a year, as the principled white abolitionist refused to discuss Johnson's rescue. Leading abolitionists such as Harriet Tubman and Frederick Douglass visited Williamson in jail, and abolitionists everywhere paid close attention to the courtroom dramas surrounding the case. Protests snowballed until Judge Kane finally relented and released Williamson from prison. Many years later Johnson wrote to her rescuer, informing Williamson that she was eternally grateful for his actions and that she was particularly happy that her sons were in school. For abolitionists and even moderate northerners, however, the message was clear: the federal government was determined to protect slavery and attack those who thwarted the Fugitive Slave Law.

African Americans and the Fugitive Slave Law

In August 1854, African Americans came to Cleveland from all corners of the country to discuss the merits and wisdom of leaving the United States. While emigrationist sentiment had waxed and waned among African Americans since the late 1700s, the final antebellum decade witnessed a strong upsurge in favor of emigration among African Americans. Just a few years before, in 1848, black Americans had met in the same city to denounce colonization, emigration, and racial exclusion, urging biracial cooperation in the fight against slavery. By the 1854 meeting, however, northern black views of emigration had changed dramatically, and there was one key reason: as far as many leading black Americans were concerned, the Fugitive Slave Law passed as part of the Compromise of 1850 had declared open season on free and fugitive African Americans alike, permitting slave hunters to capture suspected runaways with little proof, no jury trial, and no habeas corpus protections. The new law had reshaped African American intellectual culture, lending credibility to those who saw no safe future in America. "Where, then, is our hope of success in this country?" the delegates asked with a mordant tone. "[Why] do our political leaders and acknowledged great men [tell us] to be patient, remain where we are?" In other lands, the convention platform declared, there were "no prisons, nor Court Houses, as slave-pens and garrisons, to secure the fugitive and rendezvous the mercenary gangs . . . no perjured Marshals, bribed Commissioners, not hireling counsel, who, spaniel-like, crouch at the feet of Southern slave-holders."[43]

If we are to understand not just the southern sentiments that led to secession but also the equally powerful northern determination that southerners would not be allowed to secede peacefully without consequences, then we must take Schurz and other northern eyewitnesses seriously. The Fugitive Slave Law convinced northern moderates, who might have believed that slavery was merely a southern problem, that they could not sit idly by and let southerners simply walk away from the Union. As Theodore Parker declared in the wake of Minkins's recapture, "It has been said that Slavery is a thing with which the people of the Free States have nothing to do. Who shall dare . . . to come forward and pretend it now?"[44] The answer, as Parker well knew, was that such a position was increasingly untenable. Though northern Democrats would still make the argument in the 1860 election, northeastern and midwestern voters would no longer find much that was credible in Democratic claims that slavery remained merely a southern issue. And the abduction of suspected runaways within their midst convinced hordes of northern voters that political moderation and compromise with the white South required a complete rejection of deeply held humanitarian and religious principles. In this way, the Fugitive Slave Law swayed northern public opinion, weakened the Second Party System, and brought the nation closer to war.

CHAPTER FIVE

An End to Compromise

On a cold January day in 1857, a middle-aged man of community standing stood to speak before an audience roused to the point of fury with indignation. The man himself matched the anger of his listeners, and the core of his passionate rage led to one conclusion: the Union must be dissolved. Like the men and women gathered to hear him declare his support for disunion, the speaker believed that the constitutional compromise had proved to be a miserable failure, and that the only task remaining was to dissolve the national compact and let the North and South go their separate ways: "I say Liberty and Union; if it may be; Liberty first, and Union afterward, if need be. Liberty in the Union and under the Constitution if possible; but Liberty out of the Union and over the Constitution, if it must be!" The enraptured audience, responding with action, then passed a number of resolutions supporting secession. As one of these resolutions read, "The necessity of disunion is written in the whole existing character and condition of the two sections of the country—in their social organization, education, habits and laws—and no government on Earth was ever strong enough to hold together such opposing forces."[1] The convention closed with the promise to continue to rally others in the cause of disunion and to hold a series of meetings that would doom the Constitution.

At first glance, the calls for the breakup of the Union seem to fit well with what we know about southern fire-eaters who believed that the differences between North and South over slavery were too vast to save the Republic. Yet, the meeting just recounted was not held in Charleston or Richmond or New Orleans or any other southern town. The State Disunion Convention, as it was called, came to order in Worcester, and the president of the gathering was Massachusetts native Francis William Bird, a Republican friend of Charles Sumner, supporter of William Seward and Abraham Lincoln, and leading northern paper manufacturer. As his political connections suggest, Bird was not a lone defender of northern secession. In fact, Bird's call for more northern local disunion meetings was heeded by citizens in Albany and Utica and culminated in a region-wide northern secessionist meeting in Cleveland in the fall of 1857.

The Worcester meeting took root in one of the North's most divided cities. Riots had erupted throughout the 1850s, including the famous Butman affair, which had rocked Worcester just a few years prior in 1854. That particular episode had climaxed with notorious slave catcher Asa Butman run out of town and barely escaping with his life. The State Disunion Convention was largely driven by the Democrats' successful campaign for the presidency in the November 1856 elections. "The most recent Presidential Election," the organizers pessimistically declared, would likely result in "four years more of Pro-Slavery Government."[2] Unwilling to tolerate another presidential term in which northern states' rights would be trampled by the federal slave power, a power just reaffirmed by the Supreme Court's decision on the *Dred Scott* case, the speakers cried, "Our union with slavery has been all the time sapping our moral foundations" and paralyzing "the Northern conscience." Just as alarmingly, the state's borders had been continually violated by slave hunters and their federal marshals. "Let *Massachusetts* draw the line around her own borders," speaker Samuel May shouted. "Let New England draw it around *her* borders, that she may defend the slave, and no longer be his overseer."³ The convention closed with rebukes of northern politicians who acquiesced in the Fugitive Slave Law and the constitutional compromise with slaveholders.

The Worcester meeting was followed in the spring of 1857 with assemblies in upstate New York that were led by an interracial group of northerners who had decided that the federal government and its Constitution had been so twisted and warped by slaveholders that the Union was doomed to collapse. At the Utica meeting, led by African American abolitionist Charles L. Remond, about seventy people attended including Susan B. Anthony, William Lloyd Garrison, and Sarah Clark.⁴ Abolitionist speakers Abby Kelley Foster and Wendell Phillips joined the Albany meeting, which also passed resolutions seeking to sever the North's ties to the slave South.⁵ Like the initial gathering in Worcester, the New York assemblies garnered nationwide attention.

The Worcester, Utica, and Albany meetings generated calls for a broader disunion meeting that would include all the free states. Northern papers from Maine to Minnesota spread word of a national disunion convention that would take place in Cleveland in the fall of 1857.⁶ The Panic of 1857, a dramatic and devastating economic downturn that struck the country in the early months of that year, threatened to derail the plans. But there were other obstacles as well, including the reluctance of many northerners who feared that attending a disunion meeting might be akin to treason. When the Worcester organizers, including Thomas Wentworth Higginson, Wendell Philips, and Daniel Mann, mailed out a circular announcing the call for a national convention, they declared their intention "to create a united and determined North" that would provide a sectional defense against the slave power.[7] More than six thousand northerners from every free state signed the call, but the response to the circular was mixed.[8] On the one hand, responses poured in from towns and villages across the North and West; supportive messages arrived from fourteen towns in Illinois, seventeen in Indiana, twenty-one in Michigan, and scores of other locales throughout the free states. Nathaniel H. Whitney of Howland, Michigan, was reticent to support disunion, but he added, "If there is no other way to rouse our dormant manhood, and put us upon our feet again, we will spare no pains to hasten this catastrophe."[9] Another letter writer from Hunlington, Massachusetts, included the endorsements of several citizens, declaring that "most of the above names cry *down with the Union.*"[10] On the other hand, many feared that attending the meeting would be met with arrest. A New England writer admitted that folks in his town were reluctant to sign their names to the call and have it published out of apprehension that they might be jailed for treason.[11] Most respondents, however, seemed to concur with the thinking of one respondent from Richfield, New York: "Let the Union slide."[12]

The financial panic created confusion among the conference organizers, who tried to cancel the gathering in Cleveland, but so many wanted the assembly to continue despite the panic that the convention met nonetheless. Newspapers around the country reported on the meeting, some applauding the northern disunion movement and many others denouncing its efforts. Abolitionist papers like the *Anti-slavery Bugle* of Lisbon, Ohio, offered readers detailed accounts of the proceedings.[13] Others mocked the meeting as "about seventy-five Disunionists, men, women, and non-descripts, negroes and all."[14] But the attendees, who had decided to meet even though the national convention had been called off, were inspired by the speeches delivered by Parker Pillsbury, Abby Kelley Foster, and others to take back home the message of disunion. In a letter to William Lloyd Garrison, Joseph Treat of Elyria, Ohio, concluded his account of the meeting, "Yours, for making a clear end of the Union."[15]

Mainstream Republicans did not know what to make of the 1857 disunion meetings. Some, like leading Massachusetts politician Henry Wilson, were adamantly opposed to such calls. Wilson sent a carefully crafted letter to the organizers of the Worcester meeting declaring that, though he fervently shared their disdain for bondage and their frustrations with the "slave power's" control over the federal government, he could not promote the breaking up of the republic. Chicago Republicans declared, "[We are] utterly and totally opposed to the application of the remedy for existing evils, which they recommend. They are abolitionists; we are Republicans."[16] Yet the Republican *Chicago Tribune* could not draw such sharp distinctions forever, realizing that disunionists and abolitionists were an increasingly powerful voice within the party.

White southerners responded to northern calls for disunion with ridicule. Mississippi's *Hinds County Gazette* headlined its story "The Crazy Men's Meeting," while the *Baltimore Sun* denounced the "convention of madmen."[17] The irony of northerners calling for secession was not lost on southern observers, who compared the calls to the infamous Hartford convention of northern Federalists during the War of 1812. "Another Hartford Convention!" the *New Orleans Daily Creole* scoffed. "It will result much as its predecessor did."[18] After the convention concluded, another Louisiana paper predicted, "The members will go home and enjoy the blessings of peace secured to them by that Union they seek to destroy."[19]

Southern papers need not have worried, for the disunion meetings did not gain a broad following. But they do indicate that many northerners were coming to the conclusion that the Constitution was fatally flawed and that the free states could

An End to Compromise 119

not and should not remain long in a union with slaveholders. But if the end of the Republic was still not the best approach to dealing with a house divided, then what other options remained? Was there still a way to save the Union?

Compensated Emancipation

While free-state voters in the Northeast and Midwest had grown weary of the repeated violations of their states' rights, a view that led many to question the value of continuing the national compact, others continued to search for ways to compromise with slaveholders. Even committed abolitionists like Gerrit Smith and Elihu Burritt sought new paths to keep the Union intact, even as radical abolitionists like Garrison and those gathered at the Worcester disunion meeting had long abandoned any notions of preserving the Union. In 1857, the same year as northern secessionists met in New England, Burritt resurrected an idea for ending slavery that had periodically found currency as early as the American Revolution. Compensated emancipation never gained much traction as public policy in America, despite the fact that England had included compensation for slaveholders in its colonies when it abolished the institution in 1833, and other European nations had similarly offered indemnification to their colonies. The subject occasionally came before the U.S. Congress, including for a brief period during and after the controversy over Missouri's admission into the Union.[20]

Compensated emancipation garnered unprecedented attention, however, when Burritt embarked on a campaign to bring nationwide attention to his proposal. Between 1857 and 1859, Burritt was a passionate and persistent advocate of a system by which southern slaveholders would be paid for freeing enslaved property. In the early phases of his campaign, Burritt seemed to win the polite approbation of his northern audiences, which

Burritt took as encouragement. In April 1857 Burritt stopped in Burlington, Vermont, to lay his plan to sell land in the federally owned western territories and use the funds to pay $300 for each southern slave. As Burritt readily acknowledged, the specific details of his plan remained to be determined, which he thought might be accomplished with a national convention to be held at the end of August in Cleveland.

Northern Democrats and white southerners were skeptical of Burritt's proposal from the beginning. The *New Orleans Times-Picayune* ardently maintained, "We meet these movements with the explicit declaration that slavery is our business exclusively, not theirs in any degree."[21] The Democratic Party supporting the *Detroit Free Press* agreed, declaring the obvious point that slaveholders were never going to acquiesce to the proposal: "The South asks to be let alone. Let us let them alone."[22] Burritt's plan never received even a modicum of southern backing, and his free-state support was hardly more substantial.

But the undeterred Burritt nonetheless organized the national convention in Cleveland toward the end of the summer of 1857. According to one paper, there were actually more attendees on the first day than Burritt had anticipated.[23] A number of speakers questioned not just the feasibility of raising enough money to purchase nearly four million slaves but also the morality of doing so. Numerous objections were raised to the seeming justification of the ownership of human beings by participating in their purchase, even if the ultimate goal was a laudable one. Others, including William Watkins, argued that enslaved people themselves, rather than their masters, should be compensated. Watkins, born to free black parents in Baltimore in 1826, was a prominent ally of Frederick Douglass and one of the Northeast's leading abolitionists. He stood before the convention and delivered a passionate attack on compensation, pointing out that the enslaved should be first in line in any compensation plan. Others agreed. When Gerrit Smith rose to give a lengthy and rousing speech in favor of compensated emancipation, he suggested offering slaves $25 and slaveholders $150 from funds raised from western lands.[24] The selling of territories in the West was key, according to Smith, because it was land owned by the free and slave states in common and therefore northerners would be rightly contributing to the end of bondage. "The whole nation has contributed to nationalize [slavery]," Smith argued forcefully before the convention. "Northern commerce has connived at, and openly upheld, slavery. So have Northern politics." It was only right and just, Smith maintained, for northerners and midwesterners to share in the costs of abolishing the system.[25] In response to Smith's powerful speech, the convention passed a dozen resolutions in support of pursuing Burritt's proposal. After the convention, Burritt himself tried to carry the momentum via a periodical devoted to compensated emancipation called *North and South*.

Radical abolitionists like Garrison, however, thought Smith had betrayed the antislavery cause. In *The Liberator*, Garrison harshly criticized Smith for backing what he thought was an immoral and impractical plan to send hundreds of millions of federal dollars to slaveholders. After dutifully reprinting the convention's resolutions, Garrison—never one to miss a chance to engage in sectarianism—turned on Smith: "This is the latest (not the last) of the eccentricities, gyrations and somersets of Mr. Smith. . . . His step from 'the Jerry Rescue level' and alas from the position that slaveholders are 'pre-eminent pirates,' to the compensation of the southern man-stealers as a just and obligatory act on the part of the North, exceeds the stride from 'the sublime to the ridiculous.'"[26] Smith was quite hurt by Garrison's scorn and penned a letter to Samuel May expressing sadness at the attack.

Despite the lack of enthusiastic backing even among abolitionists for his emancipation plan, Burritt continued to press the free states for the next few years, traveling from town to town like an itinerant evangelical preacher to garner followers. But Burritt could not gain significant traction for his proposals. As even his limited support began to wane in 1859, a compensated emancipation meeting for New York State attracted only a dozen attendees.[27] Later that fall, Burritt gave up hope and closed his procompensation periodical.[28]

White Southerners and Federal Power

Burritt's idea for compensated emancipation would have required the federal government to undertake an unprecedented role in collecting and distributing vast funds, all with the goal of appeasing the slaveholding South. As we have seen, after the Fugitive Slave Law, free-state citizens were coming to the opinion that a powerful federal government had been commandeered for the interests of the South. A "slave power," northerners and midwesterners complained bitterly, was threatening the rights of free states to keep slavery out of their borders.

The free-soil appeal to states' rights against a domineering federal government has an interesting corollary as white southerners discussed their views on federal and state power before Lincoln's election. In fact, turning the usual historical narrative on its head, political leaders like Georgia senator Robert Toombs reminded fellow southerners that they really had had nothing to fear from the federal government for generations. On the Senate floor in January 1860, Toombs rose to deliver a lengthy speech to declare abolitionists, not the federal government, the real enemy of the white South. "We do not charge these wrongs against the Federal Government," Toombs argued. "There has been no time, since its establishment, when it has been truer to its obligations, more faithful to the Constitution, than within the last seven years." The problem according to Toombs was not that the federal government had proved unfriendly toward slavery or that it violated southern states' rights but rather that individual northern states were now seeking to contravene federal authority. In arguing that the "higher law" of states' rights rose above federal power, Massachusetts and other northern states, in Toombs' eyes, had violated the Constitution. Such states had abandoned their former willingness to abide by the national compact, placing the Union in dire jeopardy, and free-state anger over the Fugitive Slave Law openly acknowledged this crucial shift in northeastern and midwestern political culture.[29]

Lincoln's election changed Toombs' equation, for now the federal government would reside in the hands of a chief executive opposed to slavery's expansion. But before November 1860, Toombs reminded his constituents that the federal government had protected and defended bondage since 1787. He was right, of course, as northerners complained when they denounced the "slave power conspiracy" that had dominated federal law since the nation's founding. As long as federal power lay in the hands of slavery's apologists, then there was hope for the Union in the eyes of southern whites. When that power shifted, they acted on a promise to withdraw from a Union that no longer served the interests of slavery's most passionate defenders. As Toombs had warned before Lincoln's election, if antislavery Republicans captured the White House, their "possession of the Federal Government [would be] a just cause of war by the people whose safety [would be] put in jeopardy."[30]

As Toombs made clear, because of the federal government's determination to enforce the Fugitive Slave Law, and because the executive branch headed by pro-South Democrats had bent over backwards to demonstrate its willingness to protect slavery, slaveholders had little to fear from the federal government. The Republicans and their abolitionist allies, on the other hand, had reason to denounce the federal government's intrusion into free states to enforce the Fugitive Slave Law. This calculus remained throughout the 1850s and shifted only when Lincoln and the Republicans captured the executive mansion.

The Collapse of the Border

Despite this expansion of federal power in the interests of the white South, the thousand-mile border between slavery and freedom had proved impossible to police from the very beginning of the nation. Part of the reason for that difficulty was that as the nation itself grew in size and complexity, mobility across the borders became easier. For people determined to make better lives for themselves and their families, no wall or border would prevent the desire to move.

Runaways and their allies worked to erase the border between liberty and bondage throughout the 1850s and into the Civil War itself. While Kansas and Missouri had been locked in a battle over slavery since the early 1850s, that battle did not wane after the Kansas-Nebraska Act passed in 1854. On the contrary, civil conflicts that had been tearing the free states apart continued unabated. In early 1859, abolitionist John Doy took eleven runaways and two free people of color into Lawrence, Kansas, the site of a vicious raid by proslavery forces. Doy took his charges across a river in two sets of horses and wagons at two o'clock in the morning. Unfortunately for Doy and the people under his care, they were surrounded by armed men and arrested.[31] Just a year later, when the political parties were beginning to plan their campaigns for the election of 1860, another fugitive slave crisis erupted in Kansas in the Charley Fisher rescue cases.[32] By the end of 1860, shortly after Lincoln's election, one Kansas citizen declared flatly, "The Fugitive Slave Law is dead."[33]

Failure of Compromise

As we have seen, the concept of compromise, once the hallmark of American political culture, had become a byword for unprincipled acquiescence to the opposition. Clay had been hailed during his career for his ability to help craft the Missouri Compromise, and Stephen Douglas was equally credited initially as emblematic of the next generation of politicians who could form compromises with political adversaries. But soon after the ill-fated Compromise of 1850 and its despised Fugitive Slave Law infuriated northerners and southerners alike, "compromise" became tainted. Throughout the 1850s and into the first months of President Lincoln's administration, attempts at compromise between slavery and free soil either worsened tensions or had no effect at all. As William Seward had remarked scornfully, the South had learned over the nineteenth century that "freedom, which could not be conquered at once, could be yielded in successive halves by successive compromises."[34] In the view of Seward and an increasing number of like-minded free-state voters, the South had learned this lesson all too well, while the residents of the nonslave states were beginning to awaken.

Just how much the word "compromise" had become anathema among many northern voters became clear in the 1860 presidential election. Northern Democrats united around the party leader and Union supporter Stephen Douglas, while southern Democrats rallied around former vice president and strong supporter of slavery John C. Breckinridge. Free-state voters generally had two other options: Republican candidate Abraham Lincoln or Constitutional Union Party candidate John Bell. That Bell and his new party fared so poorly in the free states suggests that a simple pro-Constitution and pro-Union statement was insufficient to garner even modest support. As historian Michael Holt found, Bell garnered only a paltry seventy-eight thousand votes in northern states.[35] The Constitutional Union Party had offered a simple platform that would seem to be as noncontroversial on its face as one might imagine. The brief, two-paragraph platform pledged simply, "It is both the part of patriotism and of duty to recognize no political principle other than THE CONSTITUTION OF THE COUNTRY, THE UNION OF THE STATES, AND THE ENFORCEMENT OF THE LAWS." Who could disagree with such a statement? Apparently the vast majority of northern voters, who voted for a much stronger and clearer rejection of the slave power embodied in Lincoln and the Republicans. In fact, as I have tried to argue throughout the previous chapters, the shift in northern and western public opinion on slavery between 1800 and 1860 meant that such voters were no longer interested in compromising with the slave power and its insistence on controlling every branch of the federal government. Lincoln secured victory in every state except New Jersey, a resounding and overwhelming rejection of the Democratic Party that had devoted much of the previous half century to appeasing southern slaveholders.

Last Ditch Compromise Efforts

Despite the seemingly inevitable coming conflict, older politicians still searched for alternatives to war, particularly for a last minute effort to solve the conflict over runaways. The Crittenden Compromise proposal demonstrated just how divisive the fugitive slave crisis remained more than a decade after the passage of the Compromise of 1850. Together with resolutions addressing the domestic slave trade and the always-fraught issue of slavery's expansion into the West, the problem of fugitive slaves, personal liberty laws, and northern unwillingness to abide by the constitutional compromise on slavery took center stage in Crittenden's proposed settlement. By the time he offered the compromise in mid-December 1860, Kentucky senator John Crittenden could boast of decades of government service, and he had actively supported the Constitutional Union Party in 1860. Now the seventy-three-year-old politician recommended solutions to what he considered to be the most common complaints of the fire-eaters: that northerners had decided to ignore the Constitution's Fugitive Slave Clause and the repeated legislative attempts by Congress to maintain the border between bondage and liberty. Specifically he suggested in one of his six proposed constitutional amendments that the federal government would offer compensation to owners of fugitive slaves who had been rescued by northern antislavery activists. Furthermore, Congress could sue in federal courts any county that refused to comply with the various fugitive slave laws passed by Congress to recoup any losses incurred in compensating masters. While Crittenden's proposed amendments also addressed the slave trade, the permanence of slavery in Washington, D.C., and the possible reestablishment of the 1820 Missouri Compromise line, his recommended congressional resolutions focused on the national controversy of the self-emancipated. In fact, three of the four resolutions Crittenden proposed to Congress directly addressed the fugitive slave crisis (the fourth supported efforts to suppress the transatlantic slave trade). Crittenden wanted Congress to reaffirm that all of the fugitive slave laws from the constitutional clause to the 1850 legislation were legal and just and had to be observed by the free states whatever they might think about slavery. Further, he argued that personal liberty laws that had repeatedly passed state legislatures in the Northeast and Midwest were unconstitutional violations of the original Fugitive Slave Clause and should be instantly repealed by the states. Finally, Crittenden maintained that one of the major complaints that free-state politicians had leveled against the 1850 Fugitive Slave Law should be remedied. Since the law's enactment, free-soil citizens had objected to the fact that marshals who returned suspected runaways received more financial reward than those who found them to be free.³⁶

Crittenden's attempt to bring political leaders together was not the last bid to solve the sectional crisis before actual war broke out. In February 1861, after Lincoln's election but just prior to his inauguration, politicians, judges, and other authorities gathered one last time in search of a settlement. Known derisively as "the Old Gentlemen's Convention" because of the significant number of older leaders like former president John Tyler, the Washington meeting sought to assuage southern fears that the northern and midwestern states were eager to squash property rights in slaves. Like the Crittenden Compromise, the greatest concern among Unionists seemed to be placating southern fire-eaters as well as southern moderates who might be tempted into adopting more extreme positions on secession. Demonstrating that many northerners had already concluded that the Constitution was not worth preserving as it then stood, Michigan and Minnesota refused to send delegates to the meeting, concerned that too much would be given away to the slave states. Not surprisingly, despite the eloquence of Tyler and other Unionists, the convention failed completely to draft even a lukewarm set of resolutions that might prevent civil war. Many free-state politicians, including David Wilmot of Pennsylvania, stood firm by the "higher law" stance. To the convention, Wilmot declared that his "first allegiance [was] to the principles of truth and justice," not the Constitution or the Union as it was.³⁷

White southerners at the convention once again made clear that they were perfectly satisfied with the federal government as long as it remained under southern control, sentiments echoed in the southern secession conventions of early 1861. At Virginia's convention in Richmond, delegates did not rail against the federal government or even federal power in the abstract. Reflecting a common position, one delegate argued, "Virginia is attached to the Union as it was."[38] Of course this meant a Union headed by a strongly proslavery president. So modern neo-Confederates should remember that southern secessionists did not oppose the federal government as long as it was one of their liking. Only after Lincoln's election did white southerners bemoan the powers in Washington, like spoiled children who could no longer get their way.

Yet northern Unionists repeatedly sought ways to pacify the South, and throughout the Thirty-Sixth Congress, which began meeting in mid-December 1860 and continued into the spring of the following year, was the setting for more than two hundred proposed resolutions and constitutional amendments that might find a path to mollifying southern extremists. An amendment proposed by veteran Ohio politician Thomas Corwin would have inoculated the Constitution against any further amendments that might jeopardize the right of southerners to own slaves. The proposal passed Congress in March and was supported both by outgoing President Buchanan as well as incoming President Lincoln. Though the proposed constitutional amendment never received the required ratification of three-fourths of the remaining states in the Union, it nonetheless paralleled similar resolutions and proposed compromises that hastily appeared before the Thirty-Sixth Congress in vain attempts to preserve the Union.[39]

Conclusion

Just as they had throughout the antebellum era, black leaders pushed Lincoln, the Union, and the Republican Party during the Civil War to acknowledge fully the importance of ending slavery. As the battles began, James McCune Smith wrote to Gerrit Smith that emancipation was "the only terms by which peace can be made." Smith pushed his white abolitionist colleague to reach further than merely reconstructing the Union:

"I charge you therefore, and charge the Garrison party likewise with being unequal to the exigency of the hour."[40] Smith wanted to let his white friends know that African Americans would accept nothing less than full emancipation, and that no more ad hoc compromises with slavery, no acquiescence to being "half-free," and no new attempts to redraw borders and lines between slavery and freedom would be acceptable. This national struggle to maintain borders, the desperate attempts to draw lines that tried but failed to hem in white criminals and protect free blacks, represents the start of the American Civil War, a battle fought within towns and cities long before Fort Sumter. Indeed, for African Americans Fort Sumter represented the culmination but not the end of a long civil war over race and the meanings of freedom and citizenship.

If the acute phase of the sectional crisis began in the 1820s and reached its apex in the 1850s and 1860s, when then might we date the close of this long civil war? As Reconstruction scholars have reminded us, the struggle can hardly be said to have concluded in 1865 or even 1877, and it has become customary for historians to refer to a "Long Reconstruction" that lasted well beyond the formal withdrawal of federal troops from the South. By one measure, the battle over African American civil rights reached a new zenith in the mid-twentieth century after waxing and waning over the course of the troubled decades between Reconstruction and World War II, a devastating era of one-party rule, racial violence, and the suppression of voting and other basic rights of citizenship. "Separate but equal" saw the end of this "Long Civil War" and the start of a new period in American history marked by conservative white retrenchment. Yet even this dark period in the early twentieth century would fall, as a newly revived movement would assert black claims to citizenship and freedom against the iron-fisted rule of violent white criminals like the Ku Klux Klan and the White League. In what scholars have come to call the long civil rights movement, activists would achieve political and legal goals first sought during a similarly enduring and complex era of which the actual Civil War itself was but a part.

As a result of black Americans' ceaseless quest for freedom, and the fact that this quest complicated the ability of white political leaders to maintain the borders between freedom and slavery, the republic was imperiled from its very beginning. Rather than establishing a strong and stable democracy, the founders should be remembered for doing what politicians often do: postponing painful or politically costly decisions to future generations. Here I'm referring specifically to the fact that the Constitution guaranteed that the country would remain a house divided between freedom and slavery. By attempting to establish boundaries between free and slave soil, and by placing the burden on enforcing that border on the free states, the Constitution required future generations to police a perimeter that even at the time of the founding stretched hundreds of miles and by the early nineteenth century would run almost a thousand miles. Beginning with the founders, each generation of white political leaders tried to maintain the border through a series of fugitive slave laws that promised to return runaways. Each one of these laws would prove unenforceable. Policing this border proved impossible and was the major cause of the Civil War.

The border proved impossible to enforce because African Americans made it so. Their unquenchable desire for freedom led enslaved people to search constantly for ways to escape, and in the process they rendered the border porous and the dividing line between bondage and freedom unenforceable. The unwillingness of African Americans to abide their bondage erased the boundaries between slavery and freedom that white politicians so desperately tried to keep intact. The combination of this thirst for liberty, together with the impossibility of maintaining the wall between slavery and freedom, tore the nation apart.

That American political leaders were unable to maintain the wall does not make them a "blundering generation," nor does it necessarily lay the blame for disunion at the feet of the generation of politicians in the 1850s. In many ways, it is remarkable that the Union did not dissolve in the wake of the Fugitive Slave Law but managed to limp on precariously all the way to the spring of 1861. After all, given the conditions that began the republican experiment joining freedom and slavery together in a Frankensteinian union that somehow was supposed to control a border that stretched through a thousand miles of wilderness, that experiment was bound to be fraught, as succeeding generations were to learn.

As author Ta-Nehisi Coates has recently argued in *The Atlantic*, placing African Americans at the center of the sectional crisis enhances our understanding of the long struggle over black civil rights, a story that anchors the historical period before and after the Civil War. By broadening our perspective and redefining our periodization, we come to understand that, from the viewpoint of African Americans who experienced kidnapping, the nation remained locked in a civil war that began in earnest in the 1820s and lasted into the late nineteenth century and beyond.

The cause of disunion that underlay all of the dissension was the persistent determination on the part of enslaved people that they would flee bondage no matter the risks. They brought slavery to the doorstep of the free states, forcing those states to recognize the meaning of freedom and the meaning of states' rights in the face of a federal government equally determined to keep standing its divided house. In so doing African Americans helped northerners and westerners to question whether the constitutional compact was still worth upholding, a reevaluation of the republican experiment that would ultimately lead not just to civil war but to the Thirteenth Amendment ending slavery and to a reconstruction of the formerly divided house. The real story of American freedom lies not with the Confederate rebels or even with the Union Army; instead, it rests with the tens of thousands of self-emancipated men and women who had to be the ones to demonstrate to the founders and to succeeding generations of Americans the value of liberty.

Notes

Introduction

1. Steven Kantrowitz, *More Than Freedom: Fighting for Black Citizenship in a White Republic, 1829–1889* (New York: Penguin Press, 2012); Jim Downs, *Sick from Freedom: African-American Illness and Suffering during the Civil War and Reconstruction* (New York: Oxford University Press, 2012); Thavolia Glymph, *Out of the House of Bondage: The Transformation of the Plantation Household* (Cambridge: Cambridge University Press, 2008).

2. Benjamin Quarles, *Black Abolitionists* (New York: Oxford University Press, 1969); John Hope Franklin and Loren Schweninger, *Runaway Slaves: Rebels on the Plantation* (New York: Oxford University Press, 1999). For more recent contributions to the study of black abolitionists and self-emancipation, see Manisha Sinha, *The Slave's Cause: A History of Abolition* (New Haven: Yale University Press, 2016); Erica Armstrong Dunbar, *Never Caught: The Washingtons' Relentless Pursuit of Their Runaway Slave, Ona Judge* (New York: Atria Books, 2017); Patrick Rael, *Black Identity and Black Protest in the Antebellum North* (Chapel Hill: University of North Carolina Press, 2002).

3. In discussing the causes of the Civil War, I do not mean to say that the war *should* have been avoided; perhaps in no other way would slavery have been extinguished. There is certainly no evidence that white southerners were interested in giving the institution up; on the contrary, southern support for slavery was stronger than ever in 1861. Nor does evidence suggest that slavery was dying out as an economic system; by most markers, the white South was as prosperous in the 1850s as it ever had been. So perhaps only a war in which nearly three-quarters of a million Americans lost their lives could have abolished slavery.

4. R. J. M. Blackett, *The Captive's Quest for Freedom: Fugitive Slaves, the 1850 Fugitive Slave Law, and the Politics of Slavery* (Cambridge: Cambridge University Press, 2018); Michael Todd Landis, *Northern*

Men with Southern Loyalties: The Democratic Party and the Sectional Crisis (Cornell: Cornell University Press, 2014); Susan-Mary Grant, *North over South: Northern Nationalism and American Identity in the Antebellum Era* (Lawrence: University Press of Kansas, 2000); Leonard Richards, *The Slave Power: The Free North and Southern Domination, 1780–1860* (Baton Rouge: Louisiana State University Press, 2000).

5. Michael Woods, "'Tell Us Something about State Rights': Northern Republicans, States' Rights, and the Coming of the Civil War," *Journal of the Civil War Era* 7 (June 2017): 242–68.

6. Manisha Sinha, *The Slave's Cause: A History of Abolition* (New Haven: Yale University Press, 2016); Quarles, *Black Abolitionists*.

7. On the role of federal politicians in defending bondage, see Don E. Fehrenbacher, *The Slaveholding Republic: An Account of the United States Government's Relations to Slavery* (New York: Oxford University Press, 2001).

8. Chandra Manning, *What This Cruel War Was Over: Soldiers, Slavery, and the Civil War* (New York: Alfred A. Knopf, 2007), 3.

9. Adam I. P. Smith, *The Stormy Present: Conservatism and the Problem of Slavery in Northern Politics, 1846–1865* (Chapel Hill: University of North Carolina Press, 2017), 2–3.

10. Speech by H. Ford Douglas on the Fugitive Slave Law, *Minutes of the State Convention of the Colored Citizens of Ohio* (Columbus: E. Glover, 1851), 7.

11. David Waldstreicher, *Slavery's Constitution: From Revolution to Ratification* (New York: Hill and Wang, 2009).

12. John Ashworth, *Slavery, Capitalism and Politics in the Antebellum Republic*, vol. 2, *The Coming of the Civil War, 1850–1861* (Cambridge: Cambridge, University Press, 2007).

13. Waldstreicher, *Slavery's Constitution*, 101.

14. Matthew Salafia, *Slavery's Borderland: Freedom and Bondage along the Ohio River* (Philadelphia: University of Pennsylvania Press, 2013), 3–7.

15. Christopher Phillips, *The Rivers Ran Backward: The Civil War and the Remaking of the American Middle Border* (New York: Oxford University Press, 2016). See also Bridget Ford, *Bonds of Union: Religion, Race, and Politics in a Civil War Borderland* (Chapel Hill: University of North Carolina Press, 2016); and Stanley Harrold, *Border War: Fighting over Slavery before the Civil War* (Chapel Hill: University of North Carolina Press, 2010).

Chapter 1. The Long Civil War

1. The details of the Seymour Cunningham story were recorded by Boston journalist and editor Joseph T. Buckingham in 1827 and later. See "Seymour Cunningham," *Freedom's Journal*, May 25, 1827, 1; and "Seymour Cunningham; or, All for Liberty," *The Liberty Bell* (Boston, 1852), 187–202.

2. Steven Hahn, *The Political Worlds of Slavery and Freedom* (Cambridge, Mass.: Harvard University Press, 2009), 5. Hahn's point that the borders between freedom and slavery are far more porous than we have previously thought forms a major theme underpinning this book. Stanley Harrold makes the point as well in *Border War: Fighting over Slavery before the Civil War* (Chapel Hill: University of North Carolina Press, 2010).

3. The meaning of "free soil" has its own complicated history. Antebellum Americans who still lived on unpaved roads and worked in farm fields identified with the importance and relevance of the land. In this chapter "free soil" means those states that had officially abolished slavery by 1800, though almost all of the emancipation measures in the North provided for a gradual end to bondage and used complicated systems of apprenticeships that extended northern slavery well into the 1800s. On the possible meanings of "free soil," see Jonathan H. Earle, *Jacksonian Antislavery and the Politics of Free Soil, 1824–1854* (Chapel Hill: University of North Carolina Press, 2004), 13–14.

4. Carol Wilson, *Freedom at Risk: The Kidnapping of Free Blacks in America, 1780–1865* (Lexington: University of Kentucky Press, 1994); David Fiske, *Solomon Northup's Kindred: The Kidnapping of Free Citizens before the Civil War* (Santa Barbara: Praeger, 2016).

5. "More Kidnapping," *The Emancipator* 4 (October 17, 1839): 99.

6. "Kidnapping," *The Emancipator* 3 (June 28, 1838): 34.

7. On the increase in domestic slave prices after 1809, see Harrold, *Border War*, 10. By 1800, states had established severe penalties for kidnapping; North Carolina and Virginia declared kidnapping a capital offense. See Ira Berlin, *Slaves without Masters: The Free Negro in the Antebellum South* (New York: New Press, 1974), 99. But such punishments failed to stem the tide of kidnapping, especially after the closing of the foreign slave trade. In her study of antebellum Louisiana, Judith Kelleher Schafer found no cases of prosecutions for kidnapping blacks despite laws against the practice. See Schafer, *Becoming Free, Remain-*

ing Free: Manumission and Enslavement in New Orleans, 1846–1862 (Baton Rouge: Louisiana State University Press, 2003). In the words of one scholar, "Once the United States had banned the international slave trade in 1808, the illegal traffic of slaves increased. More significantly, the kidnapping of blacks occurred with dramatic frequency." Stephen Middleton, *The Black Laws: Race and the Legal Process in Early Ohio* (Athens: Ohio University Press, 2005), 172. Recent examinations of the domestic slave trade, and especially the movement of hundreds of thousands of slaves from the Southeast to the Southwest, include Lacy K. Ford, *Deliver Us from Evil: The Slavery Question in the Old South* (New York: Oxford University Press, 2009); Steven Deyle, *Carry Me Back: The Domestic Slave Trade in American Life* (New York: Oxford University Press, 2005); Stephen M. Best, *The Fugitive's Properties: Law and the Poetics of Possession* (Chicago: University of Chicago Press, 2004); and Walter Johnson, *Soul by Soul: Life Inside the Antebellum Slave Market* (Cambridge, Mass.: Harvard University Press, 2000).

8. Jesse Torrey, *American Slave Trade; or, An Account of the Manner in Which the Slave Dealers Take Free People from Some of the United States of America, and Carry Them Away, and Sell Them as Slaves in Other of the States*, (Philadelphia, 1817; rpt., London, 1822), 80.

9. Paul Finkelman, *An Imperfect Union: Slavery, Federalism, and Comity* (Chapel Hill: University of North Carolina Press, 1981).

10. Berlin, *Slaves without Masters*, 99–100. See also Ira Berlin, *Many Thousands Gone: The First Two Centuries of Slavery in North America* (Cambridge, Mass.: Harvard University Press, 1998).

11. For evidence of the kidnapping of free blacks before the 1800s, see Daniel E. Meaders, ed., *Kidnappers in Philadelphia: Isaac Hopper's Tales of Oppression, 1780–1843* (Cherry Hill, N.J.: Africana Homestead Legacy Publishers, 2009); Paul Finkelman, "The Kidnapping of John Davis and the Adoption of the Fugitive Slave Law of 1793," *Journal of Southern History* 56 (August 1990): 397–422; and William R. Leslie, "A Study in the Origins of Interstate Rendition: The Big Beaver Creek Murders," *American Historical Review* 57 (October 1951): 63–76.

12. The Ohio River was the site of several escapes via steamboat. See Nikki M. Taylor, *Frontiers of Freedom: Cincinnati's Black Community, 1802–1868* (Athens: Ohio University Press, 2005), 142–43.

13. Petition Analysis Record, Chancellor of the Middle Division of Tennessee, Accession #21483709, Race and Slavery Petitions Project,

Series 2, County Court Petitions, University of North Carolina at Greensboro.

14. In discussing the importance of the Fugitive Slave Law in upholding the Union and in maintaining better feelings among the states, Nathan S. S. Beman argued that because this was "an age of increased *international communication*," southerners were well aware of northern antislavery sentiment. Beman, *Characteristics of the Age: A Discourse Delivered in the First Presbyterian Church* (Troy, N.Y., 1851), 12. On the maturation of a national postal and communication network, see Richard R. John, *Spreading the News: The American Postal System from Franklin to Morse* (Cambridge, Mass.: Harvard University Press, 1995); and David M. Henkin, *The Postal Age: The Emergence of Modern Communications in Nineteenth-Century America* (Chicago: University of Chicago Press, 2006).

15. James Brewer Stewart, "The Emergence of Racial Modernity and the Rise of the White North, 1790–1840," in *African-American Activism before the Civil War: The Freedom Struggle in the Antebellum North*, ed. Patrick Rael (New York: Routledge, 2008), 225. See also Harrold, *Border War*, 113–14.

16. *The Present State and Condition of the Free People of Color, of the City of Philadelphia* (Philadelphia, 1838), 17–21. For figures in 1860, see Rael, *African American Activism*, 1. According to Rael, the approximately 225,000 black Americans represented about 5 percent of the northern population.

17. Even when northern and midwestern states became "free soil," they established complex systems of gradual emancipation as well as apprenticeships and indentures that could be bought and sold. As a consequence, slaves remained legal in states like New Jersey well into the antebellum period. For scholarship on the fragility of freedom in the antebellum North, see Middleton, *The Black Laws*, 65; Leon Litwack, *North of Slavery: The Negro in the Free States, 1790–1860* (Chicago: University of Chicago Press, 1961); Leonard L. Richards, *Gentlemen of Property and Standing: Anti-abolition Mobs in Jacksonian America* (New York: Oxford University Press, 1970); Stanley W. Campbell, *The Slave Catchers: Enforcement of the Fugitive Slave Law, 1850–1860* (Chapel Hill: University of North Carolina Press, 1968); Gary Nash and Jean Soderlund, *Freedom by Degrees: Emancipation in Pennsylvania and Its Aftermath* (New York: Oxford University Press, 1991); Shane White, *Somewhat More Independent: The End of Slavery in New York*

City, 1770–1810 (Athens: University of Georgia Press, 1991); Joanne Pope Melish, *Disowning Slavery: Gradual Emancipation and "Race" in New England, 1780–1860* (Ithaca: Cornell University Press, 1998); Leslie M. Harris, *In the Shadow of Slavery: African Americans in New York City, 1626–1863* (Chicago: University of Chicago Press, 2003); Mark S. Weiner, *Black Trials: Citizenship from the Beginnings of Slavery to the End of Caste* (New York: Alfred A. Knopf, 2004); and Paul J. Polgar, "'To Raise Them to an Equal Participation': Early National Abolitionism, Gradual Emancipation, and the Promise of African American Citizenship," *Journal of the Early Republic* 31 (Summer 2011): 229–58. For examples of scholarship emphasizing the role of northern cities as beacons of freedom, see Richard S. Newman, "'Lucky to be Born in Pennsylvania': Free Soil, Fugitive Slaves and the Making of Pennsylvania's Anti-slavery Borderland," *Slavery & Abolition* 32 (September 2011): 413–30; and Richard S. Newman and James Mueller, *Antislavery and Abolition in Philadelphia: Emancipation and the Long Struggle for Racial Justice in the City of Brotherly Love* (Baton Rouge: Louisiana State University Press, 2011).

18. On the migration of African Americans to Canada, see Samuel Ringgold Ward, "Speech by Samuel Ringgold Ward Delivered at Freemasons' Hall, London, England, 21 June 1853," *The Black Abolitionist Papers*, vol. 1, *The British Isles, 1830–1865*, ed. C. Peter Ripley (Chapel Hill: University of North Carolina Press, 1985); and Benjamin Drew, *A North-Side View of Slavery* (Boston, 1856). For historical accounts, see Fred Landon, "The Negro Migration to Canada after the Passing of the Fugitive Slave Act," *Journal of Negro History* 5 (January 1920): 22–36; and Landon, "Social Conditions among the Negroes in Upper Canada," *Ontario Historical Society Papers and Records* 22 (1925): 1–20. Once making it to Canada, however, blacks often faced racism and discrimination. See Tony Freyer and Lyndsay Campbell, *Freedom's Conditions in the U.S.-Canadian Borderlands in the Age of Emancipation* (Durham, N.C.: Carolina Academic Press, 2011); and Jason H. Silverman, *Unwelcome Guests: Canada West's Response to American Fugitive Slaves, 1800–1865* (Millwood, N.Y.: Associated Faculty Press, 1985).

19. In this chapter, "border states" refers to those north and south of the line between slave and free soil: Pennsylvania, New Jersey, Maryland, and Delaware in the East, and Missouri, Ohio, Indiana, Illinois, Iowa, Kentucky, and the western part of Virginia in the Midwest. On defining the term "border states," see Harrold, *Border War*, xi–xii, 2–3.

20. Newman, "'Lucky to Be Born,'" 418.

21. Julie Winch, "Philadelphia and the Underground Railroad," *Pennsylvania Magazine of History and Biography* 111 (January 1987): 4, 9. For a broader sense of the region in this period, see Gabrielle M. Lanier, *The Delaware Valley in the Early Republic: Architecture, Landscape, and Regional Identity* (Baltimore: Johns Hopkins University Press, 2005).

22. As Max Grivno points out, "Free and enslaved blacks crisscrossed the Mason-Dixon Line in ways that muddied sectional differences." Grivno, *Gleanings of Freedom: Free and Slave Labor along the Mason-Dixon Line, 1790–1860* (Urbana: University of Illinois Press, 2011), 13.

23. Hal Roth, *The Monster's Handsome Face: Patty Cannon in Fiction and Fact* (Vienna, Md.: Nanticoke Books, 1998), 2. See Wilson, *Freedom at Risk*, 19–37 for a comprehensive review of the Cannon Gang's activities. See also R. W. Messenger, *Patty Cannon Administers Justice* (Cambridge, Md.: Tidewater Publishers, 1960). A brief, older account of the Cannon Gang is E. K. Williams, "Side Lights on Some of the Social Aspects of Slavery in Delaware, 1638–1865," *Negro Educational Review* 5 (January 1954): 17. Cannon's infamous activities were dramatized in a late nineteenth-century novel, George Alfred Townsend, *The Entailed Hat* (New York, 1884).

24. On politics and slavery in Maryland, see Anita Aidt Guy, *Maryland's Persistent Pursuit to End Slavery, 1850–1864* (New York: Garland Publishing, 1997); and Barbara J. Fields, *Slavery and Freedom on the Middle Ground: Maryland during the Nineteenth Century* (New Haven: Yale University Press, 1985). Grivno's *Gleanings of Freedom* also offers considerable insight into Maryland's strategic position on the border of a free state.

25. "Evils of Slavery," *Rights of All* 1 (May 29, 1829): 5.

26. Wilson, *Freedom at Risk*, 25–27.

27. Winch, "Philadelphia," 20.

28. Eric Ledell Smith, "Rescuing African American Kidnapping Victims in Philadelphia as Documented in the Joseph Watson Papers at the Historical Society of Pennsylvania," *Pennsylvania Magazine of History and Biography* 129 (July 2005): 319.

29. On race riots in Philadelphia, see Gary B. Nash, *Forging Freedom: The Formation of Philadelphia's Black Community, 1720–1840* (Cambridge, Mass.: Harvard University Press, 1988), 275–77. On Cin-

cinnati's race riots, see Middleton, *The Black Laws*; and Patrick A. Folk, "The Queen City of Mobs: Riots and Community Reaction in Cincinnati, 1788–1848" (PhD diss., University of Akron, 1978).

30. Roth, *The Monster's Handsome Face*, 59, 61–62; Smith, "Rescuing African American Kidnapping Victims," 323.

31. "Shocking Depravity," *National Gazette* (Philadelphia), April 16, 1829, 1; "Evils of Slavery," *Rights of All* 1 (May 29, 1829): 4.

32. Clinton Jackson and Erastus E. Barclay, *Narrative and Confessions of Lucretia P. Cannon, the Female Murderer* (New York, 1841). The fact that the pamphlet was published in New York more than a decade after Cannon's death testifies to the continuing interest in the case, as African Americans continued to disappear from northern free soil into the 1840s and 1850s. The *Narrative* is reprinted in Roth, *The Monster's Handsome Face*, 7–30. Cannon was alternately known as Lucretia, Martha, and Patty.

33. Roth, *The Monster's Handsome Face*, 68–76.

34. Edlie L. Wong, *Neither Fugitive nor Free: Atlantic Slavery, Freedom Suits, and the Legal Culture of Travel* (New York: New York University Press, 2009), 5.

35. Petition Analysis Record, Circuit Court of the County of St. Louis, Accession #21182704, Race and Slavery Petitions Project, Series 2, County Court Petitions, University of North Carolina at Greensboro.

36. Petition Analysis Record, Third Judicial Circuit of Missouri, Accession #21183003, Race and Slavery Petitions Project, Series 2, County Court Petitions, University of North Carolina at Greensboro.

37. Petition Analysis Record, First Judicial District Court, Orleans Parish, Louisiana, Accession #20884202, Race and Slavery Petitions Project, Series 2, County Court Petitions, University of North Carolina at Greensboro.

38. For example, see Petition Analysis Record, Circuit Court of the County of St. Louis, Accession #21183201, Race and Slavery Petitions Project, Series 2, County Court Petitions, University of North Carolina at Greensboro.

39. Petition Analysis Record, First District Court of Louisiana, Accession #20882930, Race and Slavery Petitions Project, Series 2, County Court Petitions, University of North Carolina at Greensboro (Merry); Petition Analysis Record, Circuit Court for District of Columbia, Accession #20483501, Race and Slavery Petitions Project, Series 2, County Court Petitions, University of North Carolina at Greensboro (Jenkins).

40. Petition Analysis Record, Louisville Chancery, Accession #20784508, Race and Slavery Petitions Project, Series 2, County Court Petitions, University of North Carolina at Greensboro.

41. "Controversy between Maine and Georgia," *The Emancipator* 3 (December 20, 1838): 137.

42. "Controversy between Maine and Georgia," *The Emancipator* 3 (December 20, 1838): 137.

43. W. Jeffrey Bolster, *Black Jacks: African American Seamen in the Age of Sail* (Cambridge, Mass.: Harvard University Press, 1997); Peter Linebaugh and Marcus Rediker, *The Many-Headed Hydra: Sailors, Slaves, Commoners, and the Hidden History of the Revolutionary Atlantic* (Boston: Beacon Press, 2000); David S. Cecelski, "The Shores of Freedom: The Maritime Underground Railroad in North Carolina," *North Carolina Historical Review* 71 (April 1994): 174–206.

44. Wong, *Neither Fugitive nor Free*, 184.

45. F. C. Adams, *Uncle Tom at Home: A Review of the Reviewers and Repudiators of Uncle Tom's Cabin by Mrs. Stowe* (Philadelphia, 1853), 113, quoted in Wong, *Neither Fugitive nor Free*, 185.

46. Kathryn Grover, *The Fugitive's Gibraltar: Escaping Slaves and Abolitionism in New Bedford, Massachusetts* (Amherst: University of Massachusetts Press, 2001), 78.

47. Wong, *Neither Fugitive nor Free*, 188.

48. Wong, 189.

49. "Mr. Hoar's Mission," *Southern Quarterly Review* 7 (April 1845): 467, quoted in Wong, *Neither Fugitive nor Free*, 195.

50. "Massachusetts and South Carolina," *Cincinnati Weekly Herald and Philanthropist*, December 18, 1844, 3, quoted in Wong, *Neither Fugitive nor Free*, 203.

51. Harrold, *Border War*, 79. In fact, Harrold titles chapter 4 "Interstate Diplomacy."

52. Middleton, *The Black Laws*, 164–71. See also Harold D. Tallant, *Evil Necessity: Slavery and Political Culture in Antebellum Kentucky* (Lexington: University Press of Kentucky, 2003).

53. David G. Smith, *On the Edge of Freedom: The Fugitive Slave Issue in South Central Pennsylvania, 1820–1870* (Bronx: Fordham University Press, 2012).

54. Jonathan Jennings, quoted in Matthew Salafia, *Slavery's Borderland: Freedom and Bondage along the Ohio River* (Philadelphia: University of Pennsylvania Press, 2013), 147.

55. "Resistance to the Supreme Court," *Boston Recorder* 21 (August 5, 1836): 127.

56. "Supreme Judicial Court," *Massachusetts Spy*, August 10, 1836, 2.

57. "Rescue of Slaves," *Gloucester Democrat* 2 (August 5, 1836): 3.

58. "Outrage in Court," *Niles' Weekly Register* 50 (August 6, 1836): 388.

59. "Supreme Judicial Court," *Massachusetts Spy*, August 10, 1836, 2.

60. The *Boston Centinel* observed that the action of the "lawless mob" was a "violation of the sanctuary of justice, [and] has not its parallel in the annals of the city." Quoted in "A Rescue in Court," *Alexandria Gazette*, August 8, 1836, 3.

61. "Resistance to the Supreme Court," *Boston Recorder* 21 (August 5, 1836): 127; "A Rescue in Court," *Christian Register and Boston Observer* 15 (August 6, 1836): 127.

62. William Lloyd Garrison, "Rescue of Slaves," *The Liberator* 6 (August 6, 1836): 127.

63. "A Rescue in Court," *Alexandria Gazette*, August 8, 1836, 3; "America," *Port of Spain Gazette*, October 21, 1836, 3.

64. "New York and Virginia, Another Inter-state War Impending," *The Emancipator* 4 (December 26, 1839): 137.

65. Salafia, *Slavery's Borderland*, 3, 118.

66. Christopher Phillips, *The Rivers Ran Backward: The Civil War and the Remaking of the American Middle Border* (New York: Oxford University Press, 2016), 7.

67. See Anne Marshall's important work, *Creating a Confederate Kentucky: The Lost Cause and Civil War Memory in a Border State* (Chapel Hill: University of North Carolina Press, 2010); and Aaron Astor's valuable study *Rebels on the Border: Civil War, Emancipation, and the Reconstruction of Kentucky and Missouri* (Baton Rouge: Louisiana State University Press, 2012).

68. "More Kidnapping," *The Emancipator* 1 (September 22, 1836): 82. For a case of kidnapping in Jacksonville, Illinois, see "The Illinois Kidnappers," *The Emancipator* 3 (November 22, 1838): 121.

69. "Annals of Kidnapping," *The Emancipator* 3 (July 26, 1838): 52. See also "More Kidnapping in Ohio," *The Emancipator* 3 (February 21, 1839): 174.

70. William Still, "Slave Case!" essay dated January 17, 1857, in Mary Shadd Cary Papers, Ontario Archives, Canada, reprinted in Ripley, *The Black Abolitionist Papers*, vol. 4, *The United States, 1847–*

1858, 358–61. For other examples of such deceit upon the arrest of an accused runaway, see Stephen Middleton, "The Fugitive Slave Crisis in Cincinnati, 1850–1860: Resistance, Enforcement, and Black Refugees," *Journal of Negro History* 72 (Winter/Spring 1987): 27. Underground Railroad operator William Still reported that in one instance kidnappers claimed a child was sick in order to persuade free black Thomas Hall to open his door in the middle of the night. Still, *The Underground Rail Road* (Philadelphia: Porter & Coates, 1872), 581.

71. Petition Analysis Record, Circuit Court Third Judicial Circuit, Accession #21183213, Race and Slavery Petitions Project, Series 2, County Court Petitions, University of North Carolina at Greensboro.

72. Petition Analysis Record, Circuit Court of the District of Colombia, Accession #20483702, Race and Slavery Petitions Project, Series 2, County Court Petitions, University of North Carolina at Greensboro.

73. Petition Analysis Record, Court of Common Pleas of the State of Delaware, Accession #20379611, Race and Slavery Petitions Project, Series 2, County Court Petitions, University of North Carolina at Greensboro.

74. Roger Abrahams, *African American Folktales: Stories from Black Traditions in the New World* (New York: Pantheon, 1999).

75. Kate E. R. Pickard, *The Kidnapped and the Ransomed: Recollections of Peter Still and His Wife "Vina," after Forty Years of Slavery* (Syracuse, 1856), 28, reprinted in Wong, *Neither Fugitive nor Free*, 119. Wong carefully analyzes the novel at length in chapter 2.

76. Middleton, *The Black Laws*, 94.

77. Petition Analysis Record, General Assembly of Delaware, Accession #10383702, Race and Slavery Petitions Project, Series 1, Legislative Petitions, University of North Carolina at Greensboro.

78. William R. Leslie, "The Pennsylvania Fugitive Slave Act of 1826," *Journal of Southern History* 18 (November 1852): 429–45.

79. C. B. Galbreath, "Ohio's Fugitive Slave Law," *Ohio History* 34 (1925): 217–18.

80. Earle, *Jacksonian Antislavery*, 151.

81. Leonard P. Curry, *The Free Black in Urban America, 1800–1850: The Shadow of a Dream* (Chicago: University of Chicago Press, 1981), 229.

82. Christopher Phillips, *Freedom's Port: The African American Community of Baltimore, 1790–1860* (Urbana: University of Illinois Press, 1997), 231.

83. John Brown Russwurm, "Land of Liberty," *Freedom's Journal*, December 5, 1828.

84. Jermain Wesley Loguen to Washington Hunt, December 2, 1851, reprinted in *Frederick Douglass' Paper*, April 8, 1852. See also Kellie Carter Jackson, "Force and Freedom: Black Abolitionists and the Politics of Violence, 1850–1861," (PhD diss., Columbia University, 2010), 66–97.

85. James McCune Smith to Gerrit Smith, March 31, 1855, reprinted in Ripley, *The Black Abolitionist Papers*, vol. 4, *The United States, 1847–1858*, 275.

86. William Anderson to William C. Nell, April 1860, reprinted in Ripley, *The Black Abolitionist Papers*, vol. 5, *The United States, 1859–1865*, 74–75.

87. Peter A. Browne, *A Review of the Trial, Conviction and Sentence of George F. Alberti, for Kidnapping* (Philadelphia, 1851).

88. On use of the phrase "half-free" by African Americans or by scholars to describe the northern African American experience, see William F. Cheek, *Black Resistance before the Civil War* (London: Glencoe Press, 1970), 25; Leslie M. Harris, *In the Shadow of Slavery: African Americans in New York City, 1626–1863* (Chicago: University of Chicago Press, 2003), 23–26; and Patience Essah, *A House Divided: Slavery and Emancipation in Delaware, 1638–1865* (Charlottesville: University of Virginia Press, 1996), 61, 71, 76, 81, and 104.

89. Parker quoted in Hahn, *Political Worlds*, 36. Parker was one of the key figures in the Christiana Riot in 1851, in which Maryland slave owner Edward Gorsuch and his posse went to Parker's house to recapture the escaped slaves. The definitive work on the Christiana Riot is Thomas P. Slaughter, *Bloody Dawn: The Christiana Riot and Racial Violence in the Antebellum North* (New York: Oxford University Press, 1991).

90. In the past three decades, scholars have made considerable strides in our understanding of and appreciation for the work of African American abolitionists. For excellent overviews see Steven Kantrowitz, *More Than Freedom: Fighting for Black Citizenship in a White Republic, 1829–1889* (New York: Penguin Press, 2012); Manisha Sinha, "Coming of Age: The Historiography of Black Abolitionism," in *Prophets of Protest: Reconsidering the History of American Abolitionism*, ed. Timothy Patrick McCarthy and John Stauffer (New York: New Press, 2006), 23–38; Walter C. Rucker, *The River Flows On: Black Resistance,*

Culture, and Identity in Early America (Baton Rouge: Louisiana State University Press, 2006); Patrick Rael, introduction to *African-American Activism before the Civil War: The Freedom Struggle in the Antebellum North* (New York: Routledge, 2008), 1–38. On abolitionism and African Americans, see Darryl Pinckney, "The Invisibility of Black Abolitionists," in *The Abolitionist Imagination*, ed. Andrew Delbanco et al. (Cambridge, Mass.: Harvard University Press, 2012), 109–33; Christopher Webber, *American to the Backbone: The Life of James W. C. Pennington, the Fugitive Slave Who Became One of the First Black Abolitionists* (New York: Pegasus, 2011); Graham Russell Gao Hodges, *David Ruggles: A Radical Black Abolitionist and the Underground Railroad in New York City* (Chapel Hill: University of North Carolina Press, 2010); John Stauffer, *The Black Hearts of Men: Radical Abolitionists and the Transformation of Race* (Cambridge, Mass.: Harvard University Press, 2002); Patrick Rael, *Black Identity and Black Protest in the Antebellum North* (Chapel Hill: University of North Carolina Press, 2002); Graham Russell Gao Hodges, *Slavery and Freedom in the Rural North: African Americans in Monmouth County, New Jersey, 1665–1865* (Madison: University of Wisconsin Press, 1997); Shirley J. Yee, *Black Women Abolitionists: A Study in Activism, 1828–1860* (Knoxville: University of Tennessee Press, 1992); R. J. M. Blackett, *Building an Antislavery Wall: Black Americans in the Atlantic Abolitionist Movement, 1830–1860* (Baton Rouge: Louisiana State University Press, 1983); Jane H. Pease and William H. Pease, *They Who Would Be Free: Blacks' Search for Freedom, 1830–1861* (New York: Athenaeum, 1974); and Benjamin Quarles, *Black Abolitionists* (New York: Oxford University Press, 1969).

Chapter 2. The Making of the Fugitive Slave Law and the Sectional Crisis

1. As Liz Varon has argued, cries of "disunion" carried considerable weight in the sectional dialogue. Because of the Fugitive Slave Law, many moderates in both sections found that their attempts to label reactionaries as "disunionists" carried less weight as the feasibility and desirability of compromise lessened. Elizabeth R. Varon, *Disunion! The Coming of the American Civil War, 1789–1859* (Chapel Hill: University of North Carolina Press, 2008).

2. Stanley Harrold, *Border War: Fighting over Slavery before the*

Civil War (Chapel Hill: University of North Carolina Press, 2010), 36, 47. See also Sally E. Hadden, *Slave Patrols: Law and Violence in Virginia and the Carolinas* (Cambridge, Mass.: Harvard University Press, 2001).

3. Bruce W. Eelman, *Entrepreneurs in the Southern Upcountry: Commercial Culture in Spartanburg, South Carolina, 1845–1880* (Athens: University of Georgia Press, 2008), 85, 98, 106, 109.

4. John Quist, *Restless Visionaries: The Social Roots of Antebellum Reform in Alabama and Michigan* (Baton Rouge: Louisiana State University Press, 1998), 69.

5. Delia A. Webster, *Kentucky Jurisprudence: A History of the Trial of Miss Delia A. Webster* (Vergennes, Vt., 1845). For a modern account see Randolph Runyon, *Delia Webster and the Underground Railroad* (Lexington: University Press of Kentucky, 1999).

6. According to one abolitionist newspaper account, George Latimer was "a *white* man, to the eye." "George Latimer," *Emancipator and Republican* 7 (November 3, 1842), 107. White abolitionist attorney Samuel Sewall would later declare that "his color was the same as our own." "The Great Faneuil Hall Meeting," *The Liberator* 12 (November 11, 1842): 178.

7. "The Great Faneuil Hall Meeting," *The Liberator* 12 (November 11, 1842): 178.

8. "George Latimer," *Emancipator and Republican* 7 (November 3, 1842): 106.

9. Steven Kantrowitz, *More Than Freedom: Fighting for Black Citizenship in a White Republic, 1829–1889* (New York: Penguin Press, 2012).

10. Sewall quoted in "Great Meeting for Human Rights in Faneuil Hall," *Emancipator and Republican* 7 (November 3, 1842): 107. See also "Miscellaneous," *Christian Register and Boston Observer* 21 (November 12, 1842): 184.

11. Sewall, "Great Meeting for Human Rights," 107.

12. Sewall quoted in "The Great Faneuil Hall Meeting," *The Liberator* 12 (November 11, 1842): 178.

13. James Freeman Clarke, *A Sermon Preached in Amory Hall, October 9th, 1842, Being the Sunday Succeeding the Death of William Ellery Channing* (Boston, 1842), 11.

14. "The Signs of the Times," *Latimer Journal* 1 (November 18, 1842): 3.

15. Garrison, "Our Condition as a People," *The Liberator* 12 (November 4, 1842): 175.

16. Reports in the Boston newspapers and other periodicals throughout the country pointed to the remarkable public anger and excitement Latimer's arrest generated. See, for example, "George Latimer," *Christian Reflector* 9 (November 9, 1842): 3.

17. "Report," *Latimer Journal* 1 (November 14, 1842): 2.

18. See, for example, "Re-agitation of Abolition," *Wisconsin Democrat* 1 (November 29, 1842): 3; "The Latimer Case," *New Hampshire Sentinel*, December 28, 1842, 1; and "The Case of George Latimer," *Norwich (Conn.) Courier* 21 (December 28, 1842): 2.

19. "Abolitionism Triumphant," reprinted in *Christian Reflector* 5 (December 7, 1842): 2.

20. Northern papers in turn reprinted the comments from Norfolk papers, as each side of the controversy ratcheted up the fury by reprinting and disputing each other's claims. See "The Latimer Affair," *New Bedford Register* 4 (December 14, 1842): 2; "The Latimer Case," *New York Observer and Chronicle* 20 (December 3, 1842): 195; and "The First Note from Norfolk," *The Liberator* 12 (December 2, 1842): 191.

21. "A Voice from Old Braintree," *Emancipator and Free American* 7 (December 29, 1842).

22. "Fugitives from Justice," *Philanthropist* 7 (December 7, 1842): 1–2.

23. In its annual report in 1844, the Massachusetts Anti-Slavery Society placed the Latimer case first, just before an essay on the repeal of the state's ban on interracial marriage. *Twelfth Annual Report, Presented to the Massachusetts Anti-Slavery Society* (Boston, 1844), 4–5.

24. *Speech of Mr. H. W. Hilliard, of Alabama, on the President's Message* (Washington, D.C., 1850), 6.

25. *Speech of Hon. John McQueen, of S. Carolina, on the Admission of California* (Washington, D.C., 1850), 11.

26. William Henry Trescot, *The Position and Course of the South* (Charleston, 1850), 7.

27. *Union and Freedom without Compromise. Speech of Mr. Chase, of Ohio, on Mr. Clay's Compromise Resolutions* (Washington, D.C., 1850), 16.

28. *The Slave Question. Speech of Mr. A. G. Brown, of Mississippi, in the House of Representatives, January 30, 1850* (Washington, D.C., 1850), 1.

29. *A Letter on Southern Wrongs and Southern Remedies* (Charleston, 1850), 10.

30. Meeting report quoted in *A Letter on Southern Wrongs and Southern Remedies* (Charleston, 1850), 15.

31. *Politics and the Pulpit: A Series of Articles which Appeared in the "Journal of Commerce" and in "The Independent," during the Year 1850* (New York, 1851), 5.

32. *Politics and the Pulpit*, 5.

33. "Indiana Against the Extension of Slavery," *Philadelphia Freeman* 7 (March 7, 1850): 3.

34. For a detailed account of the congressional machinations over the compromise measures, see Michael Todd Landis, *Northern Men with Southern Loyalties* (Ithaca: Cornell University Press, 2014), ch. 1.

35. *Speech of John Minor Botts, at a Dinner at Powhatan Court-House, Va.* (n.p., 1850), 5.

36. *Resolutions and Address, Adopted by the Southern Convention* (Nashville, 1850), 3.

37. *Resolutions and Address*, 4.

38. *Resolutions and Address*, 11.

39. *Resolutions and Address*, 8.

40. *Resolutions and Address*, 29.

41. DeBow, "Fugitive Slaves," *DeBow's Review* 1 (November 1850), 567–70.

42. *Speech of Mr. Soule, of Louisiana, on the Pending Measures of Compromise* (n.p., 1850), 16.

43. *Speech of Mr. Mason, of Virginia* (Washington, D.C., 1850), 12.

44. *Speech of Hon. Sam Houston, of Texas, on the Subject of Compromise* (Washington, D.C., 1850), 1.

45. *Speech of Mr. Calhoun, of South Carolina, on the Slavery Question* (Washington, D.C., 1850), 1.

46. *Speech of Mr. Calhoun*, 6.

47. *Speech of John Bell, of Tennessee, on Slavery in the United States, and the Causes of the Present Dissensions between the North and the South* (Washington, D.C., 1850), 9.

48. *Speech of John Bell*, 8–9.

49. *Speech of John Bell*, 23.

50. *Speech of the Hon. Jefferson Davis, of Mississippi, on the Measures of Compromise* (n.p., 1850), 16.

51. *Power of Congress over the Territories. Speech of Hon. Lewis Cass, of Michigan* (Washington, D.C., 1850), 1.
52. *Union and Freedom without Compromise*, 1.
53. *Union and Freedom without Compromise*, 16.
54. *Power of Congress over the Territories*, 3.
55. *Power of Congress over the Territories.*
56. *Mr. Benton's Anti-compromise Speech. Speech of Mr. Benton, of Missouri* (Washington, D.C., 1850), 15.
57. *The Union, Past and Future: How It Works, and How to Save It* (Charleston, 1850), 5.
58. *Power of Congress over the Territories*, 3.
59. William H. Gilman, ed., *The Journals and Miscellaneous Notebooks of Ralph Waldo Emerson*, vol. 11 (Cambridge, Mass.: Harvard University Press, 1975), 346.
60. Emerson, "The Fugitive Slave Law," lecture read in the Tabernacle, New York City, March 7, 1854, reprinted in Ralph Waldo Emerson, *The Works of Ralph Waldo Emerson*, vol. 11, *Miscellanies* (New York, 1909).
61. According to Holt, "the two-party system collapsed because Whig and Democratic voters lost faith in their old parties as adequate vehicles for effective political action, and they lost faith because social, economic, and political developments between 1848 and 1853 blurred the line that divided Whigs from Democrats on a host of issues." Michael F. Holt, *The Political Crisis of the 1850s* (New York: Wiley, 1978), 102. On antipartyism in the antebellum era, see Gerald Leonard, *The Invention of Party Politics: Federalism, Popular Sovereignty, and Constitutional Development in Jacksonian Illinois* (Chapel Hill: University of North Carolina Press, 2007); Mark Voss-Hubbard, *Beyond Party: Cultures of Antipartisanship in Northern Politics before the Civil War* (Baltimore: Johns Hopkins University Press, 2002); Michael A. Morrison, *Slavery and the American West: The Eclipse of Manifest Destiny* (Chapel Hill: University of North Carolina Press, 1999); Ronald P. Formisano, *The Transformation of Political Culture: Massachusetts Parties, 1790s–1840s* (New York: Oxford University Press, 1983); and Richard Hofstadter, *The Idea of a Party System: The Rise of Legitimate Opposition in the United States, 1780–1840* (Berkeley: University of California Press, 1969).
62. Quotation from speech by James W. Gerard, *The Proceedings*

of the Union Meeting, Held at Castle Garden, October 30, 1850 (New York, 1850), 14.

63. Speech of Hon. Charles Allen, at the City Hall, in Worcester, Oct. 5, 1850 (n.p., 1850), 1, 3.

64. Politics and the Pulpit, 53.

65. Arthur Dearing, "An Essay on the Fugitive Law of the U.S. Congress of 1850," printed in John W. Lewis, *The Life, Labors, and Travels of Elder Charles Bowles* (Watertown, 1852), 270, 272–73, 276.

66. Benjamin Seaver Jr. to Benjamin Seaver, February 17, 1854, Letters to Benjamin Seaver, Massachusetts Historical Society, Boston.

67. "Speech by Samuel Ringgold Ward," March 25, 1850, reprinted in *The Black Abolitionist Papers*, vol. 4, *The United States, 1847–1858*, ed. C. Peter Ripley (Chapel Hill: University of North Carolina Press, 1991), 49.

Chapter 3. Civil Conflict in the North

1. Case of Polly Negroes Memorandum, dated May 15, 1856, Salmon Chase Papers, Ohio Historical Society Archives.

2. New works on the fugitive slave crises in the 1850s include David G. Smith, *On the Edge of Freedom: The Fugitive Slave Issue in South Central Pennsylvania, 1820–1870* (Bronx: Fordham University Press, 2012); Steven Lubet, *Fugitive Justice: Runaways, Rescuers, and Slavery on Trial* (Cambridge, Mass.: Harvard University Press, 2010); Earl M. Maltz, *Fugitive Slave on Trial: The Anthony Burns Case and Abolitionist Outrage* (Lawrence: University Press of Kansas, 2010); H. Robert Baker, *The Rescue of Joshua Glover: A Fugitive Slave, the Constitution, and the Coming of the Civil War* (Athens: Ohio University Press, 2007); and Gary L. Collison, *Shadrach Minkins: From Fugitive Slave to Citizen* (Cambridge, Mass.: Harvard University Press, 1997).

3. On Chase's efforts to keep the case alive, see Salmon P. Chase to John Saidley, March 18, 1856, Salmon Chase Papers, Ohio Historical Society Archives. In this letter, Chase asked Saidley to "report to [him] from time to time" on the progress of the case, suggesting that Chase did not anticipate a quick resolution. Chase turned out to be correct, and the case continued to cause agitation between Ohio, Kentucky, and Virginia until the 1860s. For evidence of the continuing agitation, see A. M. Gangener to Ralph Seete, November 12, 1859, and S. S. Rice to

Chase, February 16, 1859, Salmon Chase Papers. Although a case of national importance in the 1850s, the Peyton Polly family kidnapping has attracted only sporadic interest from historians. One of the more detailed secondary accounts can be read in Stephen Middleton, *The Black Laws: Race and the Legal Process in Early Ohio* (Athens: Ohio University Press, 2005), 216–19. Quotation appears on p. 219.

4. L. H. Sheldon, *A Discourse Delivered April 10, 1851* (Andover, Mass., 1851), 23.

5. William C. Whitcomb, *A Discourse on the Recapture of Fugitive Slaves* (Boston, 1850), 8.

6. "The Fugitive Slave Bill," *Illinois State Register*, October 17, 1850.

7. Tiya Miles, *The Dawn of Detroit: A Chronicle of Slavery and Freedom in the City of the Straits* (New York: New Press, 2017).

8. George Thompson to Anne Warren Weston, March 7, 1851, Boston Public Library, Rare Books and Manuscripts.

9. "Trumbull County, Ohio," *National Era*, December 19, 1850, 204.

10. "Grant County, Indiana," *National Era*, December 19, 1850, 204.

11. F. W. Bill, "The Fugitive Slave Law," *Zion's Herald*, December 11, 1850, 199.

12. "Public Meetings at the North," *National Era*, December 5, 1850, 196.

13. Adams Jewett, "Proceedings in Dayton, Ohio," *National Era*, November 14, 1850, 184.

14. Cave Johnson to James Buchanan, quoted in Michael Todd Landis, *Northern Men with Southern Loyalties: The Democratic Party and the Sectional Crisis* (Cornell: Cornell University Press, 2014), 34.

15. *Correspondence between Mr. Webster and His New Hampshire Neighbors* (Washington, D.C., 1850), 4, 8.

16. *Proceedings of the Union Meeting Held at Castle Garden, October 30, 1850* (New York, 1850), 3. Smaller procompromise rallies took place in towns like Greencastle, Indiana. See Charles H. Money, "The Fugitive Slave Law of 1850 in Indiana," *Indiana Magazine of History* 17 (June 1921): 169.

17. *Proceedings of the Union Meeting Held at Castle Garden*, 7.

18. *Proceedings of the Union Meeting Held at Castle Garden*, 11.

19. *Proceedings of the Union Meeting Held at Castle Garden*, 19.

20. *Proceedings of the Great Union Meeting, Held in the Large Saloon of the Chinese Museum, Philadelphia, on the 21st of November, 1850* (Philadelphia, 1850), 45.

21. George M. Dallas, *Address to the Great Union Meeting in Philadelphia, on the 21st of November, 1850* (Philadelphia, 1850), 1.

22. Dallas, *Address to the Great Union Meeting*, 5–6.

23. "Great Demonstration of Northern Servility," *Pennsylvania Freeman* 7 (November 28, 1850): 2.

24. *Proceedings of the Constitutional Meeting at Faneuil Hall, November 26, 1850* (Boston, 1850), 4.

25. Henry A. Boardman, *The American Union: A Discourse Delivered on Thursday, December 12, 1850* (Philadelphia, 1851), 30–31.

26. James A. Dorr, *Objections to the Act of Congress, Commonly Called the Fugitive Slave Law Answered* (New York, 1850), 4.

27. On race riots in Cincinnati in 1829 and 1836, see Middleton, *The Black Laws*, 70, 108.

28. James Oliver Horton and Lois E. Horton, "A Federal Assault: African Americans and the Impact of the Fugitive Slave Law of 1850," in *Slavery and the Law*, ed. Paul Finkelman (Lanham, Md.: Rowan & Littlefield, 2002), 149.

29. Deborah Weston to Anne Warren Weston, April 9, 1851, in Weston Papers, Boston Public Library.

30. Gerald G. Eggert, "The Impact of the Fugitive Slave Law on Harrisburg: A Case Study," *Pennsylvania Magazine of History and Biography* 109 (October 1985): 537–69.

31. "Incidents of the Fugitive Slave Law," *New York Evangelist*, October 31, 1850, 175.

32. "Fugitive Slave Law at Detroit," *Maine Farmer*, October 17, 1850, 3.

33. "Slave Excitement in Springfield," *Zion's Herald*, October 9, 1850, 163.

34. "The New Fugitive Slave Law," *New York Evangelist*, October 3, 1850, 159.

35. *Minutes of the State Convention of the Colored Citizens of Ohio* (Columbus, 1851), 7–12.

36. William C. Nell to Amy Post, May 5, 1852, in Post Papers, University of Rochester.

37. Parker quoted in Jonathan Katz, *Resistance at Christiana* (New

York: Thomas Y. Crowell Co., 1974), 87. The definitive account of the Christiana affair is Thomas P. Slaughter's *Bloody Dawn: The Christiana Riot and Racial Violence in the Antebellum North* (New York: Oxford University Press, 1991).

38. David Grimsted has argued that in American history mobs have often emerged from those in society "most clearly excluded from an equitable share of its goods and privileges." See *American Mobbing, 1828–1861* (New York: Oxford University Press, 1998), vii–viii.

39. On personal liberty laws, see Thomas D. Morris, *Southern Slavery and the Law, 1619–1860* (Chapel Hill: University of North Carolina Press, 1999); and Norman L. Rosenberg, "Personal Liberty Laws and Sectional Crisis, 1850–1861," *Civil War History* 17 (March 1971): 25–44. On *Prigg v. Pennsylvania*, see Robert M. Cover, *Justice Accused: Antislavery and the Judicial Process* (New Haven: Yale University Press, 1975), 166–74.

40. Jane H. Pease and William H. Pease, *They Who Would Be Free: Blacks' Search for Freedom, 1830–1861* (New York: Atheneum, 1974), 214–15.

41. Thomas Prentiss Ayer Diary, February 15, 1851, American Antiquarian Society. On the Minkins case, see Steven Lubet, *Fugitive Justice: Runaways, Rescuers, and Slavery on Trial* (Cambridge, Mass.: Harvard University Press, 2010), 69–60, 137–47; and Gary L. Collison, *Shadrach Minkins: From Fugitive Slave to Citizen* (Cambridge, Mass.: Harvard University Press, 1997).

42. On the struggles of African Americans in the capital city, see James Oliver Horton and Lois E. Horton, *Black Bostonians: Family Life and Community Struggle in the Antebellum North* (New York: Holmes & Meier, 1979). The Thomas Sims case has attracted considerable scholarly interest, much like the Minkins case in 1851 and the return of Anthony Burns to slavery in 1854. See, for example, Lubet, *Fugitive Justice*, 147–56. For a contemporary account of the outrage over the return of Sims, see Theodore Parker, *The Boston Kidnapping: A Discourse to Commemorate the Rendition of Thomas Sims, Delivered on the First Anniversary Thereof, April 12, 1852, before the Committee of Vigilance, at the Melodeon in Boston* (Boston, 1852).

43. "The Boston Negro Mob—The 'Higher Law' in Practice," *New-Hampshire Patriot* 4 (February 27, 1851): 2. See also "A Slave Case in Boston," *New-Hampshire Patriot* 4 (February 20, 1851): 2; and "Treason," *New-Hampshire Patriot* 4 (April 10, 1851): 2.

44. "The 'Higher-Law' Mob in the Senate," *New-Hampshire Patriot* 4 (February 27, 1851): 2.

45. "Arrest of a Kidnapper at Worcester," *New York Times*, October 31, 1854, 1.

46. Ira Berlin, *Many Thousands Gone: The First Two Centuries of Slavery in North America* (Cambridge, Mass.: Harvard University Press, 1998), 283, 320 (quotation).

47. *Trial of Rev. John B. Mahan, for Felony* (Cincinnati, 1838), 3. For an excellent online exhibit on freedom papers, see "Free at Last? Slavery in Pittsburgh in the 18th and 19th Centuries," University of Pittsburgh Library, accessed November 29, 2018.

48. Loguen, *Rev. J.W. Loguen's Answer to the Theology of the Rev. H. Mattison* (Syracuse, 1856), 33–36.

49. See the section "Kidnapping under the Law," in *Fourteenth Annual Report, Presented to the Pennsylvania Anti-slavery Society* (Philadelphia, 1851), 32–34.

50. For a general statement of the practice, see the *Freedom's Journal*, March 7, 1827, 2. On the prohibition of black testimony in court, see Ira Berlin, *Slaves without Masters: The Free Negro in the Antebellum South* (New York: New Press, 1974), 100.

51. According to historian Nikki M. Taylor, "the 1850 Fugitive Slave Act made it easier to kidnap free blacks with impunity." Nikki M. Taylor, *Frontiers of Freedom: Cincinnati's Black Community, 1802–1868* (Athens: Ohio University Press, 2005), 155.

52. Money, "The Fugitive Slave Law of 1850 in Indiana," 179.

53. Kathryn Grover, *Make a Way Somehow: African-American Life in a Northern Community, 1790–1965* (Syracuse: Syracuse University Press, 1994), 33. One Virginian lamented in 1850 that "kidnapping is the order of the day." Berlin, *Slaves without Masters*, 161.

54. Historians are recognizing the important evolution of a northern states' rights ideology. See, for example, Michael E. Woods, "'Tell Us Something about State Rights': Northern Republicans, States' Rights, and the Coming of the Civil War," *Journal of the Civil War Era* 7 (June 2017): 242–68. Woods argues persuasively that a states' rights ideology in the free states became central to Republican Party defense against the federal government's attempt to enforce the Fugitive Slave Law, particularly after 1854. See also the informative essay by Joseph A. Ranney, "'Suffering the Agonies of their Righteousness': The Rise and Fall of the

States' Rights Movement in Wisconsin, 1854–1861," *Wisconsin Magazine of History* 75 (Winter 1991–92): 82–116.

55. Dallas, *Address to the Great Union Meeting in Philadelphia*, 5.
56. *Proceedings of the Union Meeting Held at Castle Garden*, 28.
57. Kazlitt Arvine, *Our Duty to the Fugitive Slave* (Boston 1850), 31.

Chapter 4. Trying to Save the Union

1. Holt generally denies the centrality of slavery to the sectional crisis in *The Political Crisis of the 1850s* (New York: Wiley, 1978); see especially pp. 2–5. Holt also argues, "National party commitments to the Compromise in the short run meant an end to the fierce interparty conflicts over the Fugitive Slave Law that had characterized Northern state politics in 1850, 1851, and 1852, prior to the presidential campaign" (p. 98).

2. Michael Todd Landis, *Northern Men with Southern Loyalties: The Democratic Party and the Sectional Crisis* (Cornell: Cornell University Press, 2014), 100.

3. On challenges to planter hegemony in the antebellum South, see Jonathan Daniel Wells and Jennifer R. Green, *The Southern Middle Class in the Long Nineteenth Century* (Baton Rouge: Louisiana State University Press, 2011); Bruce W. Eelman, *Entrepreneurs in the Southern Upcountry: Commercial Culture in Spartanburg, South Carolina, 1845–1880* (Athens: University of Georgia Press, 2008); Jonathan Daniel Wells, *The Origins of the Southern Middle Class, 1800–1861* (Chapel Hill: University of North Carolina Press, 2004); Jennifer R. Green, *Military Education and the Emerging Middle Class in the Old South* (Cambridge: Cambridge University Press, 2008); Frank J. Byrne, *Becoming Bourgeois: Merchant Culture in the South, 1820–1865* (Lexington: University Press of Kentucky, 2006); and Tom Downey, *Planting a Capitalist South: Masters, Merchants, and Manufacturers in the Southern Interior, 1790–1860* (Baton Rouge: Louisiana State University Press, 2006).

4. R. J. M. Blackett, *Beating against the Barriers: The Lives of Six Nineteenth-Century Afro-Americans* (Baton Rouge: Louisiana State University Press, 1986), 41.

5. Benjamin Quarles, *Black Abolitionists* (New York: Oxford University Press, 1969), 19. See also Julie Roy Jeffrey, *The Great Silent Army of Abolitionism: Ordinary Women in the Antislavery Movement* (Chapel Hill: University of North Carolina Press, 1998).

6. Quarles, 215.

7. Patrick Rael, *Black Identity and Black Protest in the Antebellum North* (Chapel Hill: University of North Carolina Press, 2002), 51.

8. "Convention of the Colored Citizens of Gallia County," *Frederick Douglass' Paper*, January 1, 1852, 1.

9. James Brewer Stewart, *Holy Warriors: The Abolitionists and American Slavery* (rev. ed., New York: Hill and Wang, 1997), 137, 157. See also Gary L. Collison, *Shadrach Minkins: From Fugitive Slave to Citizen* (Cambridge, Mass.: Harvard University Press, 1997), ch. 5; and Walter C. Rucker, *The River Flows On: Black Resistance, Culture, and Identity Formation in Early America* (Baton Rouge: Louisiana State University Press, 2006).

10. *Proceedings of the State Convention of Colored People at Albany, New York, on the 22nd, 23rd, and 24th of July, 1851* (Albany, 1851), 29.

11. On the vigilance committees in Syracuse and Rochester, see "Proceedings of a Meeting of Rochester Blacks" in *The Black Abolitionist Papers*, vol. 4, *The United States, 1847–1858*, ed. C. Peter Ripley (Chapel Hill: University of North Carolina Press, 1991), 98.

12. William P. Newman to Frederick Douglass, October 1, 1850, reprinted in Ripley, *The Black Abolitionist Papers*, vol. 4, *The United States, 1847–1858*, 64.

13. Evidence of such heightened rhetoric abounds. See, for example: Kristen Tegtmeier Oertel, *Bleeding Borders: Race, Gender, and Violence in Pre–Civil War Kansas* (Baton Rouge: Louisiana State University Press, 2009), 52–55; and John Stauffer, *The Black Hearts of Men: Radical Abolitionists and the Transformation of Race* (Cambridge, Mass., 2001), ch. 1.

14. State personal liberty laws passed in the early 1840s tried to thwart efforts to enlist state government help or to hold runaways in state facilities. Thomas D. Morris, *Free Men All: The Personal Liberty Laws of the North, 1780–1861* (Baltimore: Johns Hopkins University Press, 1974).

15. Carl Schurz, *Life of Henry Clay*, vol. 2 (Boston, 1891), 371.

16. Jermain Wesley Loguen to Frederick Douglass, August 11, 1851, reprinted in Ripley, *The Black Abolitionist Papers*, vol. 4, *The United States, 1847–1858*, 86.

17. Schurz, *Life of Henry Clay*, 375.

18. "Meeting of the Citizens of New Bern," *Frederick Douglass' Paper*, December 4, 1851.

19. Outlaw quoted in William W. Freehling, *The Road to Disunion*, vol. 1 (New York: Oxford University Press, 2007), 504.

20. *Speech of Hon. Langdon Cheves, of South Carolina, in the Southern Convention, at Nashville, Tenn., November 14, 1850* (Charleston, 1850), 2.

21. Robert F. Lucid, ed., *The Journal of Richard Henry Dana, Jr.*, vol. 2 (Cambridge, Mass.: Harvard University Press, 1968), 410.

22. Lucid, 412.

23. Lucid, 420.

24. John Hope Franklin and Loren Schweninger, *Runaway Slaves: Rebels on the Plantation* (Oxford: Oxford University Press, 1999), 149, 162.

25. Caphart quoted in *Boston Commonwealth* (June 19, 1851), n.p.

26. Description quoted in *Boston Commonwealth* (February 21, 1851), n.p.

27. *Journal of the State Convention* (Milledgeville, Ga., 1850), 15.

28. Jonathan Katz, *Resistance at Christiana* (New York: Thomas Y. Crowell, 1974), 89–90.

29. H. Robert Baker, *The Rescue of Joshua Glover: A Fugitive Slave, the Constitution, and the Coming of the Civil War* (Athens: Ohio University Press, 2007).

30. "The Slave Trade," *The Liberator*, July 7, 1854.

31. "Sensible Views from a Southern Paper on State Rights," *National Era*, October 26, 1854.

32. "Sensible Views from a Southern Paper on State Rights," *National Era*, October 26, 1854.

33. "The Fugitive Slave Act—Proposition for Its Repeal," *Louisville Journal*, August 31, 1854.

34. *The Liberator*, August 25, 1854.

35. "Wilmot at Home," *National Era*, August 31, 1854.

36. "Slave-Catching in Vermont," *The Liberator*, December 15, 1854.

37. "Senator Douglas's Reception in Chicago," *Frederick Douglass' Paper*, September 15, 1854.

38. *The Liberator*, March 10, 1854.

39. On the centrality of foreign policy and slavery's expansion to Democratic Party politics in the 1850s, see Landis, *Northern Men with Southern Loyalties*, ch. 4.

40. On the role of southern politicians in the Kansas-Nebraska controversy, see Alice Elizabeth Malavasic, *The F Street Mess: How South-*

ern Senators Rewrote the Kansas-Nebraska Act (Chapel Hill: University of North Carolina Press, 2017).

41. On the furious anger directed toward Douglas, see Landis, *Northern Men with Southern Loyalties*, pp. 120–127. For the Douglas quotation see p. 128.

42. Section 28 established the same rules for Kansas.

43. *Proceedings of the National Emigration Convention of Colored People, 1854* (Pittsburgh, 1854), 60, 69.

44. Boston circular written by Parker, March 10, 1851, in Theodore Parker Scrapbook, Boston Public Library.

Chapter 5. An End to Compromise

1. *Proceedings of the State Disunion Convention* (Boston, 1857), 11, 12.

2. *Proceedings of the State Disunion Convention*, 3.

3. *Proceedings of the State Disunion Convention*, 15, 16.

4. "Convention of Radical Abolitionists," *New York Tribune*, February 17, 1857. 5. For a detailed, if jaundiced, view of the proceedings, see "The Disunion Convention at Utica," *New York Herald*, February 22, 1857, 2.

5. "Disunion Convention in Albany," *New Orleans Times-Picayune*, February 7, 1857, 1.

6. See, for example, "The Disunion Convention," *St. Paul Daily Pioneer*, January 31, 1857, 2. This paper was highly critical of the meeting, referring to the gathering as a plan "to plot treason and rebellion."

7. Thomas Wentworth Higginson, *Call for a Northern Convention* (Worcester, Mass., 1857), 3.

8. "Disunion Convention," *New-Hampshire Patriot*, September 30, 1857, 2.

9. Nathaniel H. Whitney to Thomas Wentworth Higginson, September 13, 1857, Slavery in the U.S. Collection, box 2, folder 7, American Antiquarian Society.

10. See the responses from Massachusetts, Slavery in the U.S. Collection, box 2, folder 6, American Antiquarian Society.

11. At least one correspondent manifested this concern. See the Slavery in the U.S. Collection, box 2, folder 8, American Antiquarian Society.

12. Unnamed correspondent from New York, Slavery in the U.S. Collection, box 2, folder 17, American Antiquarian Society.

13. "The Disunion Convention," *Anti-slavery Bugle*, October 31, 1857, 3; "Northern Disunion Convention," *The Liberator*, November 13, 1857, 182.

14. "The Disunion Convention," *New Albany Daily Ledger*, November 4, 1857, 3.

15. "Disunion Convention at Cleveland," *The Liberator*, October 30, 1857, 175.

16. "A Disunion Convention," *Chicago Tribune*, September 29, 1857, 2.

17. "The Crazy Men's Meeting," *Hinds County Gazette*, January 14, 1857, 2; "Disunion Convention in Massachusetts," *Baltimore Sun*, December 31, 1856, 1.

18. "Disunion Convention," *New Orleans Daily Creole*, December 18, 1856, 2.

19. "A National Disunion Convention," *Baton Rouge Daily Gazette and Comet*, August 14, 1857, 2. See also "National Disunion Convention," *Nashville Union and Banner*, July 10, 1857, 2.

20. On the tortured history of compensated emancipation in America, see Betty L. Fladeland, "Compensated Emancipation: A Rejected Alternative," *Journal of Southern History* 42 (May 1976): 169–186.

21. "Officious Philanthropy," *New Orleans Times-Picayune*, August 13, 1857, 2.

22. "Compensated Emancipation," *Detroit Free Press*, June 24, 1857, 2.

23. "From Cleveland," *New York Tribune*, August 28, 1857, 5.

24. Manisha Sinha, *The Slave's Cause: A History of Abolition* (New Haven: Yale University Press, 2016), 549–50.

25. "Compensated Emancipation," *Anti-slavery Bugle*, October 31, 1857, 1.

26. William Lloyd Garrison, "Compensation Emancipation Convention," *The Liberator*, September 4, 1857, 3.

27. "Compensated Emancipation Convention," *Cleveland Daily Leader*, February 1, 1859, 1.

28. "The News," *The Tennessean*, September 22, 1859, 2.

29. Robert Toombs, *Invasion of States: Speech Delivered in the Senate* (Washington, 1860), 2, 7.

30. Toombs, *Invasion of States*, 3.

31. Ephraim Nute to unidentified recipient, February 14, 1859, Kansas Memory, accessed June 24, 2017, www.kansasmemory.org

/item/4933/text. See also Mary Brown to William Brown, January 30, 1859, Kansas Memory, accessed June 25, 2017, www.kansasmemory.org/item/3399/text. Doy recounted fully his participation in the episode: *The Narrative of John Doy* (New York, 1860). For a valuable analysis of the fugitive slave crisis in another western state, see Lowell J. Soike, *Busy in the Cause: Iowa, the Free-State Struggle in the West, and the Prelude to the Civil War* (Lincoln: University of Nebraska Press, 2014).

32. See Thomas Ewing Jr. to Thomas Ewing Sr., April 21, 1860, Kansas Historical Society, accessed June 25, 2017, www.kshs.org/archives/935.

33. James Montgomery to George L. Stearns, December 12, 1860, Kansas Memory, accessed June 25, 2017, www.kansasmemory.org/item/90536/text.

34. Leonard L. Richards, *The Slave Power: The Free North and Southern Domination* (Baton Rouge: Louisiana State University Press, 2000), 10.

35. Michael F. Holt, *The Political Crisis of the 1850s* (New York: Wiley, 1978), 215.

36. For a comprehensive examination of Crittenden and his proposed compromise, see Michael D. Robinson, *A Union Indivisible: Secession and the Politics of Slavery in the Border South* (Chapel Hill: University of North Carolina Press, 2017); and Damon R. Eubank, *In the Shadow of the Patriarch: The John J. Crittenden Family in War and Peace* (Macon: Mercer University Press, 2009).

37. Wilmot quoted in Mark Tooley, *The Peace That Almost Was* (Nashville: Nelson Books, 2015), 208. Tooley's account of the meeting is a valuable and thorough record of the politicians and their machinations.

38. Tooley, 189. See also pp. 212–13.

39. On the Corwin amendment and Lincoln's support for the law, see Daniel W. Crofts, *Lincoln and the Politics of Slavery: The Other Thirteenth Amendment and the Struggle to Save the Union* (Chapel Hill: University of North Carolina Press, 2016).

40. James McCune Smith to Gerrit Smith, August 22, 1861, reprinted in *The Black Abolitionist Papers*, vol. 4, *The United States, 1847–1858*, ed. C. Peter Ripley (Chapel Hill: University of North Carolina Press, 1991).

Index

Abbott, Asa, 36
abolitionism: southern reaction to, 63–64; southern white response to, 51
abolitionist press: on dissolution conventions, 118; on interstate crises, 28; on kidnappings, 18–19, 36–37, 41; on Latimer case, 48; and self-emancipation, stories of, 104; on states' rights, 106. *See also individual newspapers*
Adams, S. H., 31
African American activism, 30–33, 40–41, 81–82, 86–87, 132–34. *See also* mobbing; self-emancipation; vigilance committees
Allen, Charles, 69
Anderson, William, 41
antiabolitionist sentiment, 40
antikidnapping laws, 107
Anti-slavery Bugle, 118
Arvine, Kazlitt, 89
Ashworth, John, 9
Attucks, Crispus, 99

Bedney, Joseph, 26
Bell, John, 63–64, 126–27
Benton, Thomas Hart, 66
Berlin, Ira, 22
Bird, Francis William, 116
Blackett, R. J. M., 4

Boardman, Henry A., 79
Booth, Sherman, 105–6
borders between slave and free states: and border war, 11–12; and interstate crises, 27–28; and labor, 34–35; mobility across, ease of, 125; and policing of, difficulty of, 11, 20, 30, 132–33; as porous, 17–18, 20, 27–28, 117; and transportation revolution, 27
border states, redefined, 140n19
Boston: and abolitionism, 45–50; and Burns affair, 99–101; and Minkins affair, 96–99; and mobbing, 30, 83–84; procompromise rallies, 79
Botts, John Minor, 56–57
Breckinridge, John C., 126
Brown, Albert Gallatin, 54
Brown, Henry "Box," 10
Brown, John, 3
Brown, Michael, 38
Buchanan, A. M., 26
Buchanan, James, 77–78, 130
Burns, Anthony, 94, 99–101
Burns, John, 36–37
Burritt, Elihu, 120–23
Butman, Asa O., 85, 116

Calhoun, John C., 57, 62–63
California, 60–63
Campbell, David, 33–34

Index 163

Canada, 22, 87–88, 92, 99, 104–5
Cannon, Martha "Patty," 23–24
Caphart, John, 100–101
Caribbean, 92, 109
Caroline (freewoman), 26–27
Carpenter, William, 46
Carr, Henry, 23
Cass, Lewis, 65, 66, 67–68, 77, 83
Chase, Salmon P., 53, 65–66, 67, 71, 85, 152–53n3
Cheves, Langdon, 95–96
Chicago, 80, 107–8
Christiana Riot, 146n89
citizenship: and enslaved, exclusion from, 52, 80; and free blacks, 18, 41, 42; legal rights of, 74
civil rights movement, 131–32
Clarke, James Freeman, 48
Clay, Henry, 3, 51, 60, 66, 84–85, 126
Cleveland, compensated emancipation convention in, 121–22
Clingman, Thomas, 67
Coates, Ta-Nehisi, 133
Cohen, Isaac, 36
colonization, 91–92, 112–13
Comfort (freewoman), 39
Committee of Thirteen, 59, 66
communication revolution, 21, 73, 93
compensated emancipation, 120–23
compromise, impossibility of, 126–27
Compromise of 1820, 109
Compromise of 1850: and California, 60–63; congressional debates over, 53–60, 63–66; newspaper reports on, 55–56; and sectional tensions, worsening of, 3; southern support for, 54. *See also* Fugitive Slave Law
Constitution: as flawed document, 7, 132–33; as proslavery document, 8–10, 82. *See also* Fugitive Slave Clause, nullification of
Constitutional Convention, 7–8
Constitutional Union Party, 63, 126–27, 128
Convention of the Colored Citizens, 92
Cooper, James, 77
Cooper, John, 39–40
Cooper, Lidia, 39–40
Corwin, Thomas, 130
court system: and African Americans, 12, 31–32, 38, 85, 87; and Fugitive Slave Law (1850), 17, 25–27, 74, 80
Craft, Ellen, 90, 94
Craft, William, 90, 94
Crittenden, John, 127–29
Crittenden Compromise, 127–29
Cuba, 109
Cunningham, Seymour, 14–17
Curtis, Thomas B., 79

Dallas, George M., 78
Dana, Richard Henry, 96–100; *Two Years before the Mast*, 97
Davis, Jefferson, 64
Dawson, William Crosby, 65
Day, William Howard, 82
Dearing, Arthur, 69–70
DeBow, James B., 59–60
Delany, Martin, 92
Democrats: on compensated emancipation, 121; and expansion of slavery, 109

164 Index

Democrats, northern, 107, 126; on slavery as southern issue, 113–14
Democrats, southern, 126
Dennison, Charles, 37
Detroit, 81, 83
Devall, Samuel, 36
dissolution conventions, 115–17; responses to, 118–20
disunionists, 147n1
Dodge, Augustus, 109
domestic slave trade, 19
Dorr, James A., 80
Douglas, H. Ford, 8, 82
Douglas, Stephen, 56, 66, 80, 85, 107–8, 109, 126
Douglass, Frederick, 104, 112
Doy, John, 125
Dred Scott, 3, 116

Earle, Jonathan, 40
election of 1860, 126–27
emancipation, 130–31
Emancipator, The, 18–19, 36–37
Emancipator and Republican, 46
Emerson, Ralph Waldo, 68
Evansville, Ind., 35–36

federal government: northerners' relationship with, 72, 115–20; southern whites' relationship with, 63, 123–25. *See also* Constitution; slave power conspiracy
Federalist Papers, The, 7
Fillmore, Millard, 84
Finkelman, Paul, 19–20
Fisher, Charley, 125
Foote, Henry, 64
Foster, Abby Kelley, 117
free black populations, 21–22
freedom, desire for, 14–17

freedom and slavery, debate over, 28
freedom papers, 15–16, 25–27, 30, 36, 38, 86
Freedom's Journal, 41
free labor, 52–53
free soil, 137n3, 139n17
Free-Soil Party, 97
Fugitive Slave Clause, nullification of, 33–34, 47, 67
Fugitive Slave Law (1793), 67
Fugitive Slave Law (1850): and abolitionism, increase of, 68–70, 73–74, 94–95; compared with earlier laws, 107; congressional debates over, 67–68; and enslaved people defiance of, 10; as final straw, 133; and "freedom," meaning of, 13; and legal rights, circumvention of, 80; and North as implicated in institution of slavery, 68, 88–89, 113–14; and northern identity, 107–8; nullification of, 5–6, 74–75, 88–89, 105–6; procompromise rallies, 76–81; repeal, movement for, 106–8; and sectional tensions, worsening of, 4, 13, 43–45

Gadsden Purchase, 108
Garner, Margaret, 110–11
Garnett, Henry, 90
Garrison, William Lloyd, 32–33, 48, 91–92, 108, 122
gender, and women behaving as men, 23
Gerard, James W., 77
Glover, Joshua, 104–5
Gorsuch, Edward, 83, 102–4, 146n89

gradual emancipation, 139n17
Gray, James, 45–46
Grayson, William J., 54
Great Union Demonstration (New York), 76–77
Great Union Meeting (Philadelphia), 77–78
Greeley, Horace, 41

Hahn, Steven, 17
Hall, Thomas, 145n70
Hamlet, James, 90, 94
Harrisburg, Pa., 80–81
Harrold, Stanley, 44
Hartford convention, 119
Hayden, Lewis, 99
Henry, William, 85
Higginson, Thomas Wentworth, 117
"Higher Law" speech, 66, 68
Hilliard, H. W., 51
Hoar, Samuel, 29
Holt, Michael, 69, 126–27
Houston, Sam, 62
Hunt, Washington, 41

indentured servitude, 139n17
Independence Mall, 1
Independent, The, 55–56, 69
inevitability of Civil War, 34

Jenkins, Jones H., 26
Jennings, Jonathan, 30
Jerry (alias William Henry), 85
Jewett, Adams, 75
Jim Crow era, 131
Johnson, Abraham, 103
Johnson, Jane, 1–2, 111–12
Johnson, Joseph, 23
Journal of Commerce, 55–56

Kane, John Kintzing, 112
Kansas, 106
Kansas-Nebraska Act, 3, 109–10
Kidnapped and the Ransomed, The (Pickard), 39
kidnappings: of children, 20, 22; and Fugitive Slave Law (1850), 87; and interstate crises, 23–24; and "laundering" of African Americans, 20, 25; laws against, 137n7; methods of, 37–40; prevalence of, 11, 18–20, 87–88; recovery of victims, 23–24; stories of, 71–72, 94 (see also *individual victims*); threat of, 17–18; and transportation revolution, 20; warning systems for, 83–84; in West, 35–37; white authorities as indifferent, 21, 23–25, 40–41, 88. See also mobbing

Lamkins, Jeptha, 25
Latimer, George, 45–50
Latimer, Rebecca, 45
Latimer Journal, 48
Liberator, The, 46, 48, 106, 108, 122
liberty laws, 6, 45, 83, 107, 128, 158n14
Lincoln, Abraham, 3, 126, 130; election of, 124–25, 127, 130
Loguen, Jermain Wesley, 41, 85, 86–87, 94
"long Civil War," 21, 131

Madison, James, 7
Mahala (freewoman), 38
Mann, Daniel, 117
Manning, Chandra, 6

Mason, James M., 59, 61
Massachusetts Anti-Slavery Society, 149n23
Massachusetts General Colored Association, 47
Mattison, H., 86
May, Samuel, 117
McQueen, John, 52
Merry, John, 26
Mexico, 92
Miles, Tiya, 73
Minkins, Shadrach, 83–84, 94, 96–99
Missouri Compromise, 34, 61
Mitchell, Martin, 38
mobbing, 31–33, 46, 83–85, 98–99
Moore, II. D., 81
Morris, John B., 31
Morris, Robert, 98
Mott, Lucretia, 112

National Era, 106
Negro Seamen Acts, 28–30
Nell, William C., 41, 46–47, 82
Newman, Richard S., 22
Newman, William P., 93
newspapers, 54–56. *See also* abolitionist press
North and South, 122–23
northern businesses and slave South, 76–77, 78–79, 122
Northup, Solomon, 11
Northwest Ordinance, 65

O'Conor, Charles, 77
Ohio River valley, 34–36
"Old Gentlemen's Convention," 129
Outlaw, David, 95

Panic of 1857, 117, 118
Parker, Theodore, 113
Parker, William, 42, 83, 102–4
passing, 45
Patten, Anna, 30–33
Patterson (captain), 36
Pennington, James W. C., 91
Pennsylvania Abolition Society (PAS), 22, 23
Philadelphia, 22–24, 77–78, 81, 111–12
Philadelphia Antislavery Society, 111
Phillips, Christopher, 34–35
Phillips, Wendell, 117
Pickard, Kate E. R., 39
Polly, Peyton, 71–72
popular sovereignty, 62, 106
postal service, 21
Prigg v. Pennsylvania (1842), 67, 83
procompromise rallies, 76–77, 76–81, 77–78, 79

Quarles, Benjamin, 91

race riots, 24, 80
Rael, Patrick, 92
Ralph (freeman), 25–26
Reconstruction, 131
Reid, Walker, 86
Remond, Charles L., 47, 117
Republican Party, 105, 119, 124–25, 126
Richardson, William, 39
Rochester Anti-Fugitive Slave Law Committee, 82
Russwurm, John Brown, 41

Salafia, Matthew, 11, 34–35

Schurz, Carl, 94–95
Scomp, Samuel, 24
Scott, Thomas, 92
Seaver, Benjamin, 70
secession, 52, 53–54, 95, 110, 113–14; and dissolution conventions, 115–20
Second Party System, 43, 68–70, 114
seizures. *See* kidnappings
self-emancipation: methods used, 10; monetary value lost to South, 59–60, 67; and passing, 45; and politicians' inability to control, 10; prevalence of, 9, 59–60, 132–34; slave owners' surprise by, 101–2, 103; strategies for, 86, 93, 103–4 (*see also* mobbing)
Sewall, Samuel E., 31–33, 47, 148n6
Seward, William Henry, 33–34, 41, 48, 58–59, 66, 67–68, 126
Shaw, Lemuel, 31–33, 46
Sheldon, L. H., 72
ships: and escapes, 20, 25, 45; and kidnappings, 20, 36–37
Sims, Thomas, 84, 94
Singleton, John, 25
slave agents, 14–17, 21, 22, 23–24, 25, 100–102
slave insurrections, 28–29, 50
slave power conspiracy, 4, 109, 111–12, 116, 123, 127
Small, Eliza, 30–33
Smith, Adam I. P., 7
Smith, Gerrit, 41, 122, 130–31
Smith, James McCune, 41, 130–31
Smith, Thomas, 39
Society for the Protection of Free People of Color, 41

Soule, Pierre, 61
State Disunion Convention (Worcester, Mass.), 115–17
states' rights, redefined, 88–89
Stewart, James Brewer, 21
Still, William, 1, 38, 111–12
Sumner, Charles, 52, 107

Taylor, Zachary, 51, 61
telegraph, 21, 73, 93
Thirteenth Amendment, 134
Thompson, George, 73–74
Ticknor, George, 97
Tiffin, Henry, 38
Toombs, Robert, 123–25
Torrey, Jesse, 19
trains, 104
transportation revolution, 20, 27, 37
Treat, Joseph, 119
Treaty of Guadalupe Hidalgo, 51
Trescot, William Henry, 52–53
trickster tales, 39
Tubman, Harriet, 112
Turner, Mathew, 30–32
Turner, Nat, 5, 50
Two Years before the Mast (Dana), 97
Tyler, John, 129

Unionists, 75–81, 84–85, 86–87, 106
U.S.-Mexican War, 51, 53, 108

Vesey, Denmark, 28
vigilance committees, 44, 82–83, 100, 111

Waldstreicher, David, 9
Ward, Samuel Ringgold, 70
warning systems, 93, 103
Warren, John C., 79

watch patrols, 41
Watkins, William, 121–22
Watson, Joseph, 23–24
Webster, Daniel, 56, 66, 75–76, 77, 84, 108
Webster, Delia, 44
westward expansion, 3, 51, 54, 56–59, 109–10
Wheeler, John, 111–12
Whitcomb, William C., 73
Whitney, Nathaniel H., 118
Williamson, Passmore, 1, 102–3
Wilmot, David, 129
Wilmot Proviso, 53, 56
Wilson, Henry, 119
Winch, Julie, 22
Wong, Edlie, 28
Wood, George, 76
Woods, Michael, 5

Selected books from the Mercer University Lamar Memorial Lectures

The Brown Decision, Jim Crow, and Southern Identity
James C. Cobb

Teaching Equality: Black Schools in the Age of Jim Crow
Adam Fairclough

Becoming Confederates: Paths to a New National Loyalty
Gary W. Gallagher

A Consuming Fire: The Fall of the Confederacy in the Mind of the White Christian South
Eugene D. Genovese

Moses, Jesus, and the Trickster in the Evangelical South
Paul Harvey

George Washington and the American Military Tradition
Don Higginbotham

South to the Future: An American Region in the Twenty-First Century
Edited by Fred Hobson

The Countercultural South
Jack Temple Kirby

Singing Cowboys and Musical Mountaineers: Southern Culture and the Roots of Country Music
Bill C. Malone

"Mixed Blood" Indians: Racial Construction in the Early South
Theda Perdue

Camille, 1969: Histories of a Hurricane
Mark M. Smith

Blind No More: African American Resistance, Free-Soil Politics, and the Coming of the Civil War
Jonathan Daniel Wells

Weathering the Storm: Inside Winslow Homer's Gulf Stream
Peter H. Wood

www.ingramcontent.com/pod-product-compliance
Lightning Source LLC
Chambersburg PA
CBHW010927180426
43192CB00043B/2785